that would be one
— Richardo...

PUNDEMONIUM

PUNDEMONIUM

The Step-by-Schlep

Guide to

Humour's Lowest Form

PAUL CLARKE AND JOAN SAUERS

William Heinemann Australia

Published 1996 by William Heinemann Australia
a part of Reed Books Australia
22 Salmon Street, Port Melbourne, Victoria 3207
a division of Reed International Books Australia Pty Limited
Reprinted 1996

Typeset in New Baskerville by MACKENZIES
Printed and bound in Australia by Australian Print Group

Text illustrations by Rosanna Vecchio

National Library of Australia
cataloguing-in-publication data:

Clarke, Paul, 1961–
Pundemonium: the step-by-schlep guide
to humour's lowest form.

Bibliography.
ISBN 0 85561 694 6.

I. Puns and punning. I. Sauers, Joan.
II. Title.

808.7

CONTENTS

ACKNOWLEDGEMENTS

The authors would like to thank the following for their insults—we mean input—and enthusiasm:

Jenny Morris, Jennifer Byrne, Deborah Callaghan (our goddess/publisher), Beryl Clarke-Marchi, Robert Cockburn, Rose Creswell, Don Anderson, Stuart MacFarlane, Bella Morris-Clarke, Hugh Morris-Clarke, Philip Mortlock, Penelope Tree, Robert J. Seidman, Amanda Bilson, William Zinsser, John Pinder, Annabel Blackett, Walter Redfern for leading the way, Frankie Rubenstein for his analysis of Shakespeare's sexual puns, and Ruby Heery.

ALL FOR PUN AND FUN FOR ALL

How We Got Into This Fine Mess

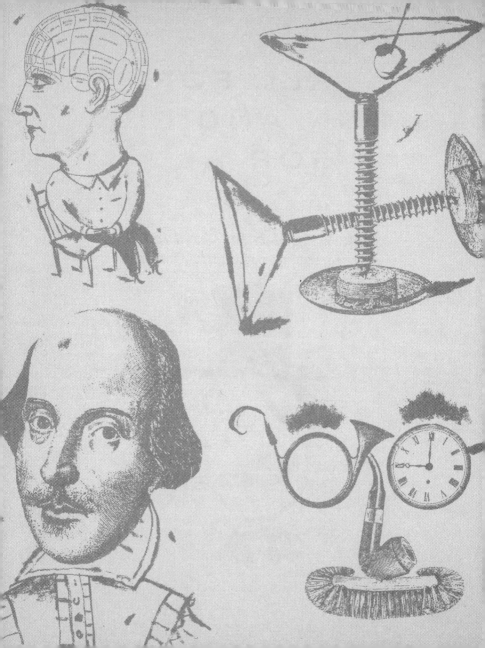

Picture this: dinner for eight at a tasteful home in Sydney's eastern suburbs. Cerebral classical music playing on the stereo. High-class wine being poured into heirloom glasses. God knows how *we* got invited. But luckily we were, because until that night we were strangers.

The group was pretty sophisticated—a Jungian analyst, a major international publisher, a Pulitzer prize-winner, a curator for a big art museum—and the conversation flitted with ease from political unrest in Tibet to Martin Amis's latest book deal. The host/analyst opened a couple of bottles of wine as dinner was served and then something happened.

Paul said to the host, 'So, the people you treat are the Jung and the restless?'

There was a momentary silence as people decided whether or not they had heard him right.

Then Joan said, 'And easily Freudened?'

The Pulitzer prize-winner looked at the napkin in her lap. The art curator excused himself to make a phone call.

Paul piped up, 'I'm sure most of them once were worriers.'

As we both laughed like drains, our host suggested sitting us at opposite ends of the table. Nothing like a couple of wise-cracking dickheads to lower the tone of a lovely dinner party. The conversation loosened up, Marley replaced Mahler on the stereo and things got cookin'. About five hours later we were still chucking puns back and forth over the kitchen table and licking Stolichnaya off the floor. Partners in grime.

Some time later, we ran into each other at a fancy dress party. Grown-ups in costume is a shocking thing, but we coped with the help of vast quantities of wine. And lots of puns. When a publisher joined us she got caught in the punning crossfire. She didn't have a chance. We aggressively suggested with the false confidence of inebriates that a book about puns was a great idea. A week later, we had signed a contract to explore what is commonly described as humour's lowest form.

At first we pretended that this was going to be easy. All we had to do was crack a bottle of something and let the puns fly. But this would be no mere dictionary of puns. Our book proposal promised a review of the pun in the history of culture from the Sumerians to *Get Smart*. We finally admitted it wasn't going to be a cakewalk, but we were excited about reading all those books we'd avoided in high school.

The first revelation was the library. It's full of really nice people whose sole job is to help you find the books you need. And it is a *great* pick-up place—better than the beach, better even than the supermarket! But the amazing thing about the library is all those books. Suddenly we realised that we could actually spend the rest of our lives researching our little tome. Punning in ancient Egypt. The use of the pun in Javanese fertility rituals. Puns seem to have wormed their way into every aspect of civilisation since the Bronze Age, and it was our job to pull it all together in a funny and informative way. Yikes. We took a step back and looked at the Big Picture. It was scary. We repaired to the pub to decide how to approach our once featherweight, now gargantuan task. A project that began in shallow drunkenness soon descended into the Literary Lost Weekend.

Obviously, there was only one thing to do. Wing it. We used our noses to follow the trail of the pun in a fairly chaotic way. It was pundemonium. Combing ancient and modern texts, movies and TV shows, we dug up a whole bunch of references to and examples of the pun, picked out our favourite stuff, and dumped the rest. So it's a motley assortment of bits and pieces we present, using sources as diverse as the Bible and the Smashing Pumpkins. The process was hit and myth.

This isn't intended as a scholarly work. Who wants to end up overweight and smelly with no friends anyway? Instead, it is a book full of wild conjecture, half-truths, dangerous advice and some factual information. And in the spirit of the pun, no concessions have been made to taste. Or political correctness. We believe you shouldn't revise history unless you're part of the ruling junta.

Occasionally we have used words of more than one syllable, many of which are located in the glossary at the back. As far as the alphabetised puns go, they have been remembered, invented, overheard, mugged, and twisted. As T.S. Eliot said, 'The bad poet borrows, the good poet steals.' And the punster will bloody well get away with what he can. After all, moral responsibility and wit are in opposite corners of life's boxing ring.

For us, writing this book has been a journey of discovery. We found out that some tracts were as good or better than we remembered. Others weren't. And sometimes, we finally figured out what the writer was on about, especially through his puns. And now that we're done, we're going to open a bottle of something to celebrate. So beer with us.

THE PUNDAMENTAL THINGS APPLY

✦

A Pun by any Other Name

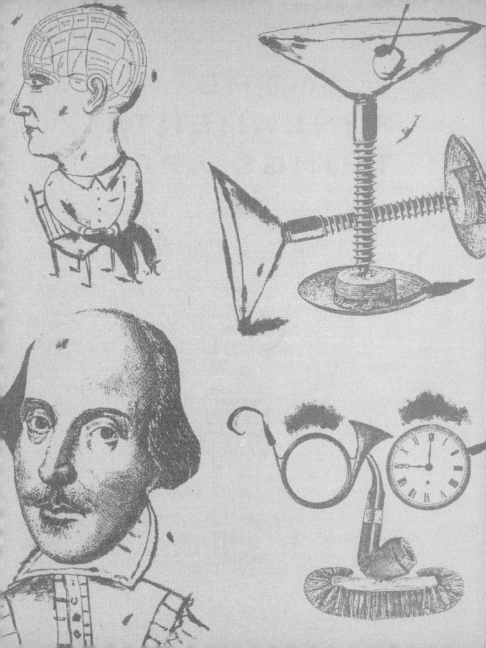

pun: the use of a word in such a way as to suggest two or more meanings ... or the use of two or more words of the same or nearly the same sound with different meanings, so as to produce a humorous effect; a play on words.

The Oxford English Dictionary

Everybody knows what it is, but no two dictionaries can agree on a definition of the pun. Some dictionaries take the easy way out and describe it simply as a play on words. Too broad. The *American Dictionary of the English Language* is more specific but gets nasty, calling it '... an expression in which a word has at once different meanings; an expression in which two different applications of a word present an odd or ludicrous idea … a low species of wit'. What do they know?

One thing is for sure: like sex and nasal hair, puns are a fact of life. They've been around since people started expanding on the grunt, and they're not going away. And like politics and religion, puns divide people. You either love 'em or hate 'em. But before we investigate the prose and cons, let's look a little closer at the anatomy of a pun. And pay attention. There *will* be a test.

The Penguin Dictionary of Literary Terms expands on and contradicts other definitions. It calls the pun 'a figure of speech which involves a play on words … often intended humorously but not always'. It mentions the Greek term for pun, *paranomasia* (from which we get **paranomaniac**, a word describing incurable pun-abusers) which refers to words that have the same sound but different meaning. For example, 'She was only a fisherman's daughter, but when she saw his rod she reeled.' This type of pun is also called a **homographic** or a **homonymic** pun because the words are spelled and pronounced the same but have multiple meanings. Some pun-theorists say that the homograph is not actually a pun but merely a homonymic play on words, because of the similar etymology. Frankly, we think this is splitting hairs (slitting pairs? hitting spares? spitting pears?). In any case, the homograph is different from another kind of pun, the **paragram**. The paragram, also known as the **paronym**, is a play on words effected by changing a letter or two, and is probably the most common type of pun. Like the one about the girl who was wasn't looking for a guy with a lot of money, just one who's tall, dark and has some. Or, the guy who looked through an old *Playboy*, taking a walk down mammary lane. (Insert groan here.)

There are infinite permutations of the pun and they've each got a ten-dollar word to describe them. There's the **asteismus**. Gesundheit! Thank you. The asteismus is a reply to an earlier word used in a different sense to convey two meanings. Like this one from *Cymbeline* written by the Grand High Wizard of Wordplay, William Shakespeare:

> Cloten: Would he had been one of my rank!
> Lord: To have smell'd like a fool.

And then there's one some cunning linguists call the **meld pun**—a word created by partly overlapping two words which share a syllable. Like the one used to describe Christmas and New Years: alcoholidays. Or the fear of fat men in red suits: Santaclaustrophobia. The meld pun is similar but not identical to the **portmanteau** word, which is a result of combining rather than overlapping words, like 'brunch'. It was best defined by Humpty Dumpty in Lewis Carroll's *Alice Through the Looking Glass*:

> Humpty: Well, 'slithy' means 'lithe' and 'slimy' … You see it's
>   like a portmanteau—there are two meanings packed
>   up into one word.

If you don't know what portmanteau means, look it up.

Somebody went to the trouble of making up the term **antanaclasis**, so we'd better tell you what it is. It's a kind of extended pun which repeats the same word with a different meaning. Like when that old pun-meister, Goethe, said, 'Experience is only half of experience.' Or when Benjamin Franklin quipped, 'We must all hang together, or assuredly we shall all hang separately.' Or how about those too true words from another presidential punster, Calvin Coolidge: 'The business of America is business.' The antanaclasis is also called an **equivoque**, exemplified by this epitaph for a bank teller: 'He checked his cash, cashed in his checks and left his window. Who is next?' Yet another term for this trope (a figure of speech, in case you haven't checked the glossary) is **ploce**. Once again, simply the use of a word in first a general, then a specific sense. Or vice versa. Twentieth-century pun king, James Joyce, used it when he talked about people who were 'more Irish than the Irish'. The Bible—that Noah's Ark of arcane linguistic forms— was big on the ploce. In Romans Paul suggests that, 'They are not all Israel, which are of Israel.' Hmm. By the way, if you suffer from insomnia, just read this chapter three times before bedtime.

The antanaclasis brings us to the **polyptoton**, which is *not* a Klingon bowel disorder but another repetition of words, this time in different grammatical form but with the *same* meaning. Like when Juvenal asks, 'Who shall stand guard to the guards themselves?' Robert Frost gets away with it twice in one line: 'Love is an irresistible desire to be irresistibly desired.' Such a construct has a rhetorical term all its own: **paracontapalitolyte**. Just kidding.

Chiasmus is a good one. It's not technically a pun, but is often associated with puns and known punsters. One of the best loved examples is Dorothy Parker's line to either her agent or her editor (depending on whose version you believe) on having missed a deadline: 'I'm too fucking busy and too busy fucking.' Mae West was pretty handy with the old chiasmus as well: 'It's not the men in my life that count, it's the life in my men.' It's interesting to note that while there aren't a lot of well-known women who go for the pun, they *love* a good chiasmus. What this means we have no idea, but undoubtedly some socio-linguist will blame it on gender repression. Then some bio-linguist will say women use a different part of their brain than men for language, and it bypasses the punning centre. Frankly, we *have* a life, and we're not going to spend too much time on the issue. Back to the chiasmus. Top comic punster, Groucho Marx, was able to do something which is a hanging offence in most Muslim countries; he punned within a chiasmus on a cliché. Catching sight of his former wife at a restaurant, he said, 'Marx spots the ex.' What a guy.

Moving right along, we arrive at the **malapropism**, which is effectively an unintentional pun. It's named after Mrs Malaprop, a character from R.B. Sheridan's 1775 play, *The Rivals,* in which Mrs M pretends to have greater command of the language than she does, hence her line: 'He is the very pineapple of politeness!' A more recent example was a woman overheard saying, 'I always read *Time* magazine because of the way it capsizes the week's news.' This is perhaps funnier and even closer to a true pun (though still unintentional) because the mistaken word not only sounds more like the intended word, but its meaning works within the context in a more pertinent way.

The unintentional pun is extremely common, and often even

when a pun is intended, the perpetrator will follow the quip with the tedious phrase, 'No pun intended.' This reflects the sense of universal guilt which accompanies most punning and will be addressed later. It's hard to say who would have felt guiltier when Eleanor Roosevelt asked an Oriental ambassador, 'When did you last have an election?' and he replied, 'Before blekfast.'

Believe it or not there is something called the **Tom Swifty** which is an adverbial pun and should be a hanging offence in *every* country. It doesn't get used a lot for obvious reasons: '"I'll chop the tree down," he said, lumberingly.' Or, '"No, Eve, don't make me eat that apple," he said adamantly.' Does this have something to do with Adam Ant as well as Adam? An editor once suggested a ban on adverbs and we'd recommend that the Tom Swifty be the first to go.

And then there is the **spoonerism**. The Rev. W.A. Spooner was the albino dean and warden of New College, Oxford, around the turn of the century, and was famous for transposing syllables or the first consonants between pairs of words. This is also a kind of **metathesis**. Spooner could have done this by accident or he may have suffered from a wordplay addiction, not uncommon among academics and the mentally ill. Seriously. In any case, he is probably responsible for only a fraction of the spoonerisms attributed to him. Like the time he saw a student kissing a girl in a punt and supposedly called out, 'Young man, cunts are not for pissing in!' We suspect that one is just too good to be true. More likely, although no less overwrought is his admonition to another student: 'You have tasted your worm, hissed my mystery lectures, and you must catch the first town drain.' Then there's his 'queer old dean' for 'dear old queen' which in all probability were interchangeable. And speaking of queens, he is said to have welcomed Queen Victoria to Oxford with the sentiment: 'I have in my bosom a half-warmed fish.' This conjures up a nice mental image which spoonerisms often do. In that vein, there was the usher to the theatre-goer: 'Let me sew you to your sheet.' A spoonerism *and* a pun. This trick was also mastered by the punning titan, George S. Kaufman, who mixed a neat cocktail of spoonerism, pun and cliché when told that a university friend of his daughter's had eloped: 'Ah! She put her heart before the course.' Was the guy quick or what?

Sometimes, entire words are transposed in a spoonerism, resulting in this compelling pun about alimony: bounty from the mutiny. There doesn't seem to be a separate term for this phenomenon but we're working on it, and welcome submissions from eggheads everywhere.

Another distant cousin of the pun is the **zeugma** which occurs when one verb affects more than one word or phrase, each differently. As with most of these fun-filled rhetorical devices, Dorothy Parker was very slick with the zeugma. Looking at a prospective apartment in New York, she said, '… this is much too big. All I need is room enough to lay a hat and a few friends.' If you want to alienate strangers at cocktail parties, you can also refer to the zeugma as the **syllepsis**.

There are as many more bizarre terms for different kinds of puns as there are linguists with research grants, but we're not going to give them all space here. If you're so inclined you can go to your local library and find an amazing array of books about puns wherein pedants endlessly pick at the existential implications of pleonastic (neo-plastic?) puns and the moral repercussions of the assonant ellipsis. We even came across something called the nondisambiguational pun, at which point we threw the encyclopaedia out the window and poured ourselves a Stoly. The thing is that pedantry goes against the spirit of punning. There is so much bitchiness and in-fighting among the 'experts' anyway, why not play by your own rules? Anthony Burgess decided to make up his own word to describe the pun: multiguous. A bit of a portmanteau word, perhaps, combining multi (multifaceted? multifarious? multiform?) with contiguous, it has a nice, slightly silly quality as well as being reasonably short and pronounceable. The point is that it's more important to understand the act of punning than the rhetorical terms which define it. We bet you can't name every part in your TV set but you can still get *Star Trek*. So, now that you know your ploce from your paronym (sort of), let's drop the double-talk and proceed to the heart of the pun. The part of the Hun?

ALCOHOL

When you've passed out from drinking too much,
you've gone with the binge.

Alcoholism: fighting a losing bottle.

When you were a kid you didn't like beer;
now you're older budweiser.

A rough pub is a bar for the coarse.

A guy who couldn't hold his liquor was
The Man Who Spewed Too Much.

I drink therefore I dram.

Prohibition cops: dram busters.

Anticipating that first glass of wine: Grape Expectations.

When your friends try to get you to drink more,
it's called beer pressure.

When you encounter a messy, aggressive drunk,
it's malice in chunderland.

Absinthe makes the hard grow fonder.

Homemade brew: the beer of living dangerously.

A pink elephant is a beast of bourbon.

There are two kinds of people in the world:
winners and boozers.

It wasn't the frontal lobotomy,
it was the bottle in front of me.

Tequila: the gulp of Mexico.

Non-lite beer: the bottle of the bulge.

Either way, you're covered: heads you wine, tails you booze.

A nasty drunk: beer and loathing.

A life of drinking: the long and wining road.

The pub that never closes: hops springs eternal.

Some people say drinking is bad for you,
but that's besides the pint.

You booze, you lose?

Drinking oneself to death: beer today, gone tomorrow.

Alcoholism: the days of wine and neurosis.

A hangover: bottle fatigue.

A date at the pub: bottle plan.

ANIMALS

The river gives you the benefit of the trout.

The guy who looked a lot like his pet said,
'There but for the race of dog go I.'

When the mummy horse arrives back in the corral, foals rush in.

ARABS

The sheik shall inherit the yurt.

It's dry in the desert, for Bedouin or worse.

Going to the market in Marrakesh is a bazaar experience.

ART

Someone who turns down your sculpture funding
application is a pain in the arts.

Van Gogh to Gaugin on the ephemera that is life:
ear today, gone tomorrow.

ATTITUDE

The cheek shall inherit the mirth.

AUSTRALIA

Swine, swimmin' and thongs.

Queenslander: the toad warrior.

THE HEART
OF THE PUN

Bloodlines

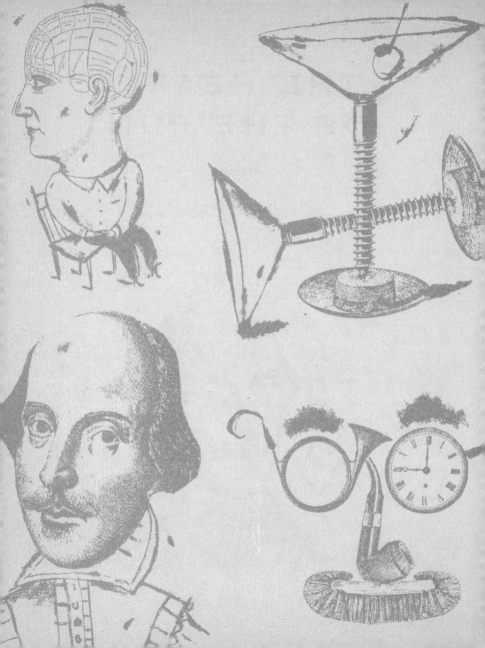

 As we delve into the essence of the pun, it's probably a good idea to see what kind of family it comes from. Not surprisingly, the etymology of the word 'pun' is murky, filled with doubt and denial from one reference book to the next. Families are like that about black sheep. Basically, 'pun' is a bastard. It was probably shortened from the Italian *puntiglio*, meaning 'a fine little point'. *Puntiglio* is a diminutive of the Latin *punctum*, meaning 'point'. A case can also be made for its origin being the verb, 'pun', which means 'to consolidate (earth, rubble) by pounding or ramming'. It's interesting that in Shakespeare's time, the term for pun was usually 'quibble', yet he

uses the word 'pun' in a sense that could mean both to pound and to pun or 'punn' as it was then spelled. In *Troilus and Cressida*, Thersites threatens: 'He would pun thee into shivers with his fist.' Obviously 'fist' suggests a physical sense, but the bard endowed his words with multiple meanings so often it's hard to say just what he intended. And victims of a pun often feel as though they have been punned in the head. Anyway, we don't think the word 'pun' derives, as Swift suggested, from the French *punaise*, which is 'a little stinking Insect, that gets into the Skin, provokes continual itching, and is with great Difficulty removed'. But you never know.

We find the first use of the word 'pun' definitely referring to wordplay in Dryden, 1662, when he writes, '… a bare Clinch will serve the turn; a Carwichet, a Quarterquibble, or a Punn'. So, clinch, quibble, fetch and carwichet or carwhitchet were all slang terms for the pun at one time. In 1676, 'pundigrion' and 'punnet' appear, which also meant pun. In 1819, Samuel Taylor Coleridge used 'punlet' to signify a wee pun. In 1866, Henry James tried out 'punkin'. A 'punnigram' refers to a punning epigram, and 'punnology' is said to be the study of puns, although we personally reject this term as sounding too much like a subject we avoided at school. 'Punnage', 'punnic', 'punnical' and apparently 'punningly' all pertain in obvious ways. The accepted terms for one-who-puns are 'punner', 'punter', and 'punster'. We like punster, as it's closest to monster, trickster, youngster, and gangster, in keeping with the personality of the pun. Whatever you do, don't mistake a pundit for a punster. The former means expert, and comes from the Hindi *pandit*, meaning teacher. Most pundits wouldn't be caught dead punning. At least in public.

Enough with lineage and on to the essence of the pun. There are as many attitudes about the pun as there are users of language, reflecting everything from adoration to disgust. Australia's reigning Prince of Puns (and exceptional for being both a pundit and a punster) is Don Anderson who put it simply: 'A pun is the shortest distance between two points; or two pints? or two punts? It is an act of linguistic economy, brevity being the soul of wit.' Here, here. Hear, hear? So, the point of a pun is its double meaning. Two for the price of one. Punsters are resourceful. They double-up, recycle, save energy, make do with what's available, invent and re-invent. In a good pun, they use two meanings whose association reveals a third meaning. The whole is greater than the sum of the parts, as in the term for a gutless cop: 'Dickless Tracy'. With a pun, we exploit the multiple personalities of words. Alexander Pope recognised the action of the pun: '… where a word, like the tongue of a jackdaw, speaks twice as much by being split'.

Puns recognise the dichotomy in words and the things they symbolise. Puns are double-jointed; they can separate meaning or join meaning, and they demand that we do the same. Our minds pivot on a pun. Mentally, we swivel. Tilt to one meaning and then back to the other. And the motion of this pivot is like a roller-coaster ride. Sometimes we laugh, sometimes we're jolted by the surprise. And sometimes we want to throw up.

The duality of a pun is its essence. It's been said that punning holds special allure for exiles—those with two homes, two languages, a dual perspective. James Joyce, Samuel Becket and Vladimir Nabokov were in that boat. In Joyce's case he spoke several languages and it still wasn't enough so he made up another, primarily comprising puns, in *Finnegans Wake*. This kind of double-take on words and ideas is automatic for punsters. It's the way they see the world. Basically, they have sick, twisted minds. As well as punning, they often use stuff like irony and paradox which also reflect two sides of the same coin. But punning in particular is aggressive and perverse. Puns bring together things meant to be kept apart, in a similar way to sexual deviance and adultery. A pun is like the embrace of two combatants in a wrestling match. In other words, punning is the art of tongue-fu.

A pun is a result of a linguistic accident—two words happen to sound alike without necessarily sharing roots. To recognise and capitalise on this accident requires an open mind. But not *just* open—malleable, loose, spontaneous. Puns are not for the control freak or the anal retentive. They are chaotic, messy, anarchic. An obscure pun is often the result of the most pathologically lateral thinking. Puns are not straightforward but they are accessible. A pun is sly, but ultimately begs to be apprehended. Puns stretch the language and challenge us to stretch our minds. They reveal and exploit the dynamic quality of words. They're iconoclastic. Liberating. Probably good for your skin. They empower us by letting us play with language as if we own it. And we do. Or at least we should. As pre-eminent pun historian and theorist Walter Redfern said, '… a pun is language on vacation'.

HOW TO PUN

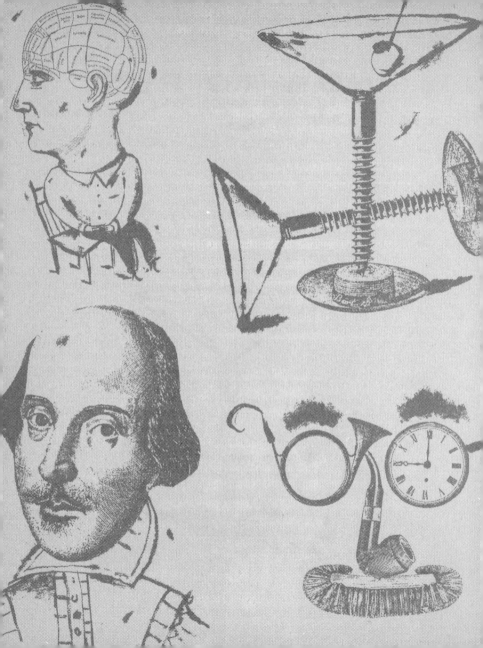

 On to the question that has plagued mankind through the ages. Can a novice learn to pun? The answer is a definite maybe. Let's put it this way—you can learn to pun but, to quote Clint Eastwood, 'A man's gotta know his limitations.' A woman should too. Children can make simple, naive puns and get away with it but adults can end up looking like dorks when they go for the LCD, or Lowest Come-On Denominator.

Nobody likes a wannabe, so if you aspire to pun greatness you have to be prepared to train for it, and we can tell you how. But be aware that some people will never be able to pun and this is not such a bad thing. Puns are like firearms; in the wrong hands they can be deadly. But if you're reading this book you must have some of the punning instinct in you. (The fact that you can read at all is a good sign.) Anyway, puns are a potent mix of highbrow, lowbrow and know-how, so let's get on to the latter. (The ladder?)

The place to start is in everyday conversation, and the first thing you have to learn is to stop thinking. If you've ever heard a would-be punster's brain ticking while he desperately tries to produce some witty gem, you'll agree it's not pleasant. You don't arrive at a pun through a measured, logical process, but rather a skewed way of seeing the world. Through a weird verbal kaleidoscope. This is the only way to come up with spontaneous puns. One way this happens is that something someone else has said will remind you in a split-second of a similar sounding word or the same word used a different way. You then create a coincidence by intentionally misunderstanding what the other person said and replacing it with your own word. You then come up with a phrase which connects both the two words and the two meanings. And you make the pun. Easy.

For instance, a friend will mention how much he or she loves mime artists, especially the 'greats' like Marcel Marceau. You will shudder at the horror of this statement, and in that moment 'mime' will become 'mind' which will lead you to a phrase which can be twisted to express your disapproval. You'll say that you feel quite the opposite: that great mimes stink alike.

The trick is to get your head in the right place for this kind of wordplay. A punster has to be alert and yet at the same time relaxed. This only seems to be a contradiction. It's like an athelete who has to be focused but not tense. Punning is a form of linguistic gymnastics. But you don't have to look good in a lycra bodysuit to do it. Thank god. Once punsters have connected two similar or same-sounding words, they become magicians, using words like trapdoors to reveal hidden meaning. You just have to start with the right attitude towards language. Make it your favourite toy. Be prepared to rough it up, make it feel good, let it think it's safe, and then eat it.

It is absolutely vital that you are able to think laterally (which doesn't mean lying down.) You have to welcome the inner voices that we all hear but don't always listen to. To do this you can do mental exercises or meditate, but some of us need that little extra something to help us on our way.

PUNDORA'S BOX

❧ or ❧

Opening the Pun-gates

For some, punning doesn't come easily in a normal state. They need a little help to get their pun juices flowing. Without outside assistance, the lid of their linguistic Pandora's box might stay closed forever.

One way to spring the lid is to hang around with known punsters. Punning can be infectious, and in willing company, puns can build on puns and be bounced back and forth like a ping-pong ball. Nothing like a game of pun-pong to loosen you up. Sometimes just knowing there are people like you around can give you the confidence to present your first paragram like, 'I beg your paronym.' For some, associating with other punsters makes them feel as if they belong to some exclusive club, but this is not to be encouraged. We recommend simple, non-judgemental bonding, like the kind that occurs between men on death row.

One of the most commonly used methods to open the doors of linguistic perception is, of course, alcohol. For centuries, drinking has been known to enhance punning, but only up to a pint, we mean point. The investigation of exactly how much booze is enough to get wordplay flowing has been turned into a science by the Irish. The nice thing about drinking, in its early stages, is that it disrupts linear thinking. Unfortunately it also disrupts linear walking, but that's another matter. A glass or two of beer or wine will make you feel less inhibited, and sometimes that's enough to get the puns rolling. There seems to be a direct effect on linguistic capability and one's sense of humour. The mind is more open to strange couplings of words and ideas which one is less fearless about uttering when residing in Margaritaville. The problem, of course, is that it is so easy to exceed critical mass.

Try this experiment at home or in the local pub: after each glass of whatever, have a sober friend keep track of the number and quality of puns you produce. It is absolutely essential that your friend not also be drinking, as your puns—even after seventeen double Armagnacs—will seem to be getting better and better until you are both admitted to hospital with acute alcohol poisoning. Several brilliant punsters have died this way, God rest their souls.

Other pun-stimulants might be safer. Baudelaire said that on hashish, people 'quite unfit for wordplay improvise endless strings of puns, highly unlikely associations of ideas, enough to drive crazy the greatest masters of this preposterous art ... The demon has got into you; it is no use resisting this hilarity which is as irksome as an itch'. We think we all know what he's talking about.

Important tip: avoid the use of cocaine as a pun-motivator. It'll be your mouth rather than your brain that gets revved up, and after a while your jaw will be so tight the puns won't have room to escape. It's what we call gnashing through the blow.

Aldous Huxley recommended using mescaline to open the trapdoors of perception, and Timothy Leary used LSD. Native

Americans use peyote, and South American natives use the coca leaf. Almost every culture on earth has used some kind of drug which has been known to induce the pun. Maybe you won't need one. In any case you'll need to be able to handle what comes next, and that's the effect of a pun.

THE BEACH

The company that brings food to you on the
shoreline is called 'Sand and Deliver'

Local sunscreen: Pacific lotion.

After a swim it's fun to lie on the sand and watch all and sun dry.

BEEKEEPING

A bee-keeper is also known as the Sultan of Sting.

Bees prefer fine weather; otherwise they like stingin' in the rain.

In a real swarm, you can't see the forest for the bees.

BESTIALITY

The most popular sheep among the farmers on a
Saturday night is a mutton for punishment.

All the farmhands want a fleece of the action.

In emergencies you'd risk life and lamb.

Feline fans like the tail of two kitties.

Your relationship with your animal is nothing to ride home about.

If you're into both male and female deers, you're Bambidextrous.

A guy's favourite piece of meat is his midnight cowtoy.

Into the equine: horse and buggery.

If you're into oral sex with felines, you have an eat-a-puss complex.

If the mare says 'neigh!', then hold your hoses.

And don't try it with an elephant or she'll take you to tusk.

If you're into small sea creatures, head down to squid row.

Sheep lover: Fleecy Rider.

The sheepdog that flirts with everyone is known as the bawdy collie.

The farmhand whispered to his favourite sheep, 'I adore ewe.'

To have sex with an animal in public is the hide of bad taste.

Husband explaining his preference to his wife:
not tonight, dear, I've got a haddock.

A choosy animal-lover likes it every which way but moose.

BETRAYAL

A traitor will double-cross that bridge when he comes to it.

BIOLOGY

When there are no toilets around you have
to exercise mind over bladder.

Ovulation: a one-night gland.

A man with a funny-looking penis has a clown-like phallus.

The Change, for some women: mean-o-pause.

The gynaecologist's office is a cervix station.

BLONDES

Marilyn Monroe in *Some Like It Hot*: the blonde leading the band.

Sharon Stone: blonde ambition.

An overweight flaxen-haired contortionist:
the blonde and winding load.

When you're obsessed with the fair-haired one, you're spellblonde.

BOWEL MOVEMENTS

The Long and Winding Load.

Stools Rush In.

When you have diarrhoea and you barely have time to get your
undies off, you get there in the knickers of time.

A Shite to Remember.

Sometimes you have to be under turd by the
bad smell coming from your shoes.

Toilet paper is for circling Uranus looking for Klingons.

Potty in your hands.

BOXING

A fixed fight: a foregone contusion.

The over-confident middleweight says to his
opponent on meeting: pleased to beat you.

After the knock-out, the victor said, 'Wallop I do now?'

THE EFFECT OF THE PUN

To pun is to take a liberty, and some people don't like that. After all, you've taken something *they've* said and twisted it to say something else. You've assigned a disguised agenda to *their* idea. Insecure people are particularly threatened by this, but should never be catered to. In fact, as with many of the perverse realities of social intercourse, punning often comes easiest and yields the most pleasure in the company of people who resist it the most. In fact some people pun for this reason alone; it's such fun to watch others squirm. Or, a pun can produce a kind of blissful agony which is almost as nice to see. Sort of like the relationship between the sadist and the masochist. This demonstrates the symbiotic, even parasitical aspect of punning.

In spite of the fact that punning exercises the mind of the victim, he or she might resent it. This is especially true when someone is taking himself too seriously. In the middle of some well-reasoned diatribe on the Weimar Republic, it's great fun to pun on one of the speaker's more earnest assertions and take the piss out of him. If the pun is particularly skilful, you might even disrupt his train of thought enough to force a change of subject. An achievement like this is up there with the multiple orgasm.

Punning is about not taking things too seriously. If you worry about hurting every single minority, interest group and religious organisation, book yourself in for some deep-sleep therapy because this is not what puns are all about. You can't be afraid to thumb your nose at authority, political correctness and everything else. Just be sure to make fun of yourself as well, and no one can ever complain. And if you find someone who considers himself free from fault, you are obliged to let him have it with both barrels. The righteous also happen to make the best targets, just begging to have that zealot's smile wiped off their face. Your job is to crack it, bruise it, paint it over, pat it on the head and send it home crying.

Remember that although it is not its primary function, the pun is extremely good at humiliating people. And the best way to deflate an ego the size of a zeppelin is casually to turn everything they say into throwaway lines. Some minor playwright might be boring everyone with his inane name-dropping, and all you have to say is, 'Your last play was very troll, it's pain to see where your talent lies.' And if it's a slow night and there aren't any major dickheads around, you just might have to pick on anybody. Make fun of their clothes, their height, their weight—whatever it takes. But, a note of warning. A pun can develop a life of its own. If you're not careful some harmless aside will come back and visit you with a couple of heavies. A good punster should be cruel but fair, which is why he will take care to unload only the best of quips, safe in the knowledge that if the line does grow a beard and have tattoos, it will still treat him kindly.

PUNSPIRATION

 ✿✿ or ✿✿

Punning on Existing Texts

Conversation is of course not the only place you find words and phrases to exercise the pun. In fact, the novice punster can build up an enormous stockpile of puns to slip into dialogue by consulting relevant reference books beforehand.

One of the most useful books in your punning library will be a rhyming dictionary which will immediately suggest thousands of puns if you can work out the right lead-in lines and context. Reading this will also get you into the habit of thinking in rhymes, which is half the job of the punster. Also, check out the works of that loquacious linguistic larrikin, Eric Partridge, who devoted his life to writing books about wordplay. Another absolute must for your reference shelf is a dictionary of clichés. Great fodder for the punster, clichés are hackneyed phrases desperate for re-interpretation. More about clichés and their importance to the punster later.

Any collection of titles like Halliwell's film and television guides will be a goldmine of memorable phrases on which to pun. The Gripes of Wrath. My Bare Lady. Live and Let Fry. A wife might like to describe her husband as For Whom The Belle Toils. Sometimes a title is already a pun on another title, like *Foetal Attraction* by Kathy Lette. Of course that's only part of the pun process. You need to come up with the right situation or context in which to use the pun. For instance, on reading through your dictionary of famous quotations before a party, you come across the line from *Hamlet*, 'There's method in his madness.'

Later that night when a friend gets royally tanked and starts telling everyone just what he thinks of them, you can comment, 'There's metho in his madness.'

Shakespeare has always been a friend of punsters, because his lines are musical, memorable, and easy to turn into a pun. Even his titles suggest endless puns. For instance, *Much Ado About Nothing* was a popular Elizabethan cliché which could be distorted thus:

When someone is boring you with tales of their gardening——

Mulch ado about nothing

A person is relating a tedious anecdote featuring their smelly dog——

Mutt ado about nothing

A harmless rodent is scaring your small daughter——

Mouse ado about nothing

A tasteless new beer is launched——

Malt ado about nothing

A vegan refuses to eat your seafood dinner——

Mussel do about nothing

A bullfight is boring——

Matador about nothing

Someone who has little to say but won't shut up——

Mouth ado about nothing

We should stop. Nah, let's keep going!

A guy won't go down on his girlfriend——

Muff ado about nothing

Some writer is giving you the shits about his latest work——

Much ado about noting

A new cookbook is published called——

Much ado about stuffing

A health scare about sheep is groundless——

Much ado about mutton

Your female parent will no longer make your bed or cook for you——

Mother do about nothing

The Greek gods are proved to be fiction——

Myth ado about nothing

You're starting to babble meaninglessly——

Mutter do about nothing

And that's just one title. Imagine how much pain and suffering you could inflict with a whole reference library!

THE CLICHE

⚛ or ⚛

Par for the Coarse

There is a deep well from which all punsters regularly draw, and that is the well of clichés. Our lives are full of them—endless rivers of platitudes and homespun wisdom ripe to be thrown on their cottage cheese arse. Hackneyed phrases are so much a part of our lives that they form valuable reference points which we all hold in common. They are so well known that people blithely accept them without realising it. Because clichés are embedded so firmly in everyone's mind, you don't need to take advantage of an accident of dialogue to get your pun off. As with Saki's elegant, simple, 'Beauty's only sin deep.' Or when Arthur Conan Doyle's brother-in-law wrote of the fictional detective, 'Tho' he might be more humble, there's no police like Holmes.'

A punster loves to turn a thing inside out—take the deep and meaningful and make it shallow, or vice versa. What could be more perfect to employ in this task than the cliché? Using a cliché means taking a tired saying, steeped in history, and applying a modern, smart-arse twist. For example, while thumbing through your dictionary of clichés you find the expression, 'salt of the earth'. Turn that baby on its head and it becomes 'slut of the earth'. Provide your own context. And if you know enough rhymes and homonyms, other offshoots will come thick and fast.

So the cliché is a foil—historical and hysterical. Chronic punsters would be nowhere near as funny without them.

Bonus points are given for lifting lines from the classics which have become clichés. Like the coward's quandary: 'To flee or not to flee, that is the question.' This is sacrilege to the Wordy Two Shoes of the planet. So it must be a good thing. And of course there are the modern classics. Lines from *Dirty Harry* do what Shakespeare once did. 'Go ahead, make my play.' The point is that you can take advantage of the fact that familiarity breeds contempt. The bottom line is, if it's been said before, say it again, only *funny* this time.

To pun on a cliché makes you look intelligent in a white trash kind of way. Listeners will be enthralled as you take some well-worn line from the Bible and relate it to being busted for drugs: 'The Lord set a narc upon Cain.' Even the little clichéd phrases that blanket our language like smog over the city can be used well. 'It's a one way street' becomes 'It's a one way sheet' when talking about limited sexual technique.

So the cliché is revered by punsters. It's not a stagnant phrase that should be banned from the language but a linguistic marathon runner, resistant, persistent and consistent. It must stand on the victory dais of Pun Olympia, flaxen-haired and proud of its achievement in sustaining wordplayers for so long. And we guarantee that, like having your first cigarette, you won't be able to stop at one cliché.

RULES OF THE RUDE

<del>≈≈≈≈≈</del> or <del>≈≈≈≈≈</del>

A Few More Guidelines

In the land of puns there are some things that just can't be taught. If somebody tells you otherwise he's lying (and probably can't pun to save his laugh). In essence, there is only one thing that must be inborn. It is, however, the Big Kahuna:

Timing

Punning genius George S. Kaufman would often say nothing for long periods during chats, merely because he was waiting for the right moment to unleash one of his multiple-impact one-liners. The ability to feel the beats of a conversation is instinctive. Seasoned wits will unconsciously clock the peaks and troughs in a *tête-à-tête* in order to gauge the perfect moment to strike. They'll be patient, never willing to waste a good line. Then it appears: the opportunity. They allow a pause. Which becomes a deathly silence. Then they drop a world-class pun from a great height, stand back, and watch the ground tremble. The huge, back-lit choir surround-sound religious experience that follows a well-timed pun is *almost* as good as that first slug of icy cold beer.

Another thing, and this is a top-shelf tip:

Never explain a pun. *Never.*

If you lay down a pun and your audience doesn't respond appropriately, just move along. You will *all* be debased by dwelling on it. Don't say 'Get it?', don't wink, don't nudge, nothing! Punsters guilty of any of these crimes should be horse-whipped. Don't even shake your head and raise your eyes to the heavens in amazement at the others' stupidity. They still won't get it but they'll hate you for making them feel like their closest ancestor is a poodle. And of course there's always the possibility that they didn't get it because it was a completely lame pun. So *you're* the moron, and you need to put that moment behind you as quickly as you can.

We also advise you to keep your ears open and steal every good line that comes your way. The pun code of ethics encourages you to do so. All those reference books might work for some, but if you've nicked your pun from someone funnier, then you have truly embraced the philosophy of the punster. Anyway, you don't want to be too studious when the back door is open and beckoning you.

So, as long as you have what it takes to begin with, and you've learned the rules of the game, you may re-enter the world wrapped in the mystique of one who puns. Punning is like being a Mason. People will know you're one but they won't know why. They'll be intrigued by how you got to be one, and would dearly like to know what you do late at night with other punsters. They'll both fear and covet your punderworld, so get used to the attention.

On the other hand, if you haven't got what it takes, you'll know about it too. The crowded kitchen at the party where you're cracking puns will be as silent as Christopher Reeves' running machine, and you might consider learning the piano accordian.

PUN AND GAMES

⚜ or ⚜

Have You Got What it Quakes?

Now that you've got the ground rules, it's time for the test. This quiz will determine whether or not you have the right attitude to be a full-time punster. Think carefully before you answer and only cheat if you have to.

1. At a party, you are talking to someone you fancy but you realise his or her partner is hovering nearby. Do you:
   (a) Excuse yourself from conversation and walk away.
   (b) Continue on, but without the attempt at seduction.
   (c) Dazzle your soon-to-be lover by saying, 'Such a shame to see the jewel with the clown,' while mocking everything the partner says.

2. The bank teller is getting on your wick by taking forever with a simple transaction. Do you:
   (a) Smile benignly while contemplating murder with a blunt excrement.
   (b) Become emasculated to the point of extinction.
   (c) Say something like, 'Time William Teller if I get out of here by tomorrow.'

3. You get pulled over by a random breath test unit. You are over the limit. Do you:

(a) Remain polite and think of something to impress the attractive officer without success.

(b) Vomit on the constable's shoes.

(c) Sing 'Police release me, let me go', and end up on a first name basis back at their place.

4. A bouncer will not let you enter a nightclub. Do you:

(a) Try hard, with no success, to slip him twenty bucks to get in.

(b) Tell him he's a dumb ox and end up in traction for a month.

(c) Say, 'This brawn cocktail needs some assalt and buttery,' which has the owner crying with laughter and letting you into the club.

5. You have to give a speech at a wedding. Your hatred of the groom is thinly veiled. Do you:

(a) Make some crack about his receding hairline (and that's about it).

(b) Stutter so babbly the bride's mother has an epilectic fit.

(c) Make a brilliant speech about the depraved sex session with the 'easy Bride, her', all the while smiling sweetly at the groom.

6. You have a fight with your lover. To resolve it do you:

(a) Make a lovely meal and try to talk it through.

(b) Sit and cry on their doorstep, snot on your lip, and beg for forgiveness.

(c) Write a stirring love letter with lines like, 'Goodness, great tits, great balls, desire,' that has them apologising and offering to give you the space you need.

7. During foreplay you ask to use a condom. The response is non-committal. Do you:

(a) Thank them for a lovely night, go home and watch porn.

(b) Blurt out that you're worried they may have the clap.

(c) Say, 'I'm not being a prophylactic of doom. I just know our sex will get down and dirty.'

8. Your boss tears strips off you in front of your colleagues. Do you:

(a) Take it on the chin, then put super-glue on his toilet seat.

(b) Wet your pants.

(c) Show your colleagues photos of your superior having sex with a donkey and say, 'Ass *him* what he's doing?'

9. You are caught going through customs in a foreign country carrying some minor contraband. Do you:

(a) Pay off the official and promise never to do it again.

(b) Allow them to strip search you and perform a rectal examination that lasts for two days.

(c) Allow them to confiscate the goods and walk, knowing that the really expensive/illegal shit has already gone through undetected, and they won't get your line anyway about 'Easy come, easy blow'.

10. Some Jehovah's Witnesses knock on your door. Do you:

(a) Tell them you're busy and close the door.

(b) Let them in and end up being baptised in the toilet.

(c) Challenge their beliefs with lines like, 'Thou shalt not bare false tit 'n' arse,' which results in them posing nude for a bikie magazine.

11. An old lover pays you a visit. Do you:

(a) Talk over the old times, think of sex, but leave well enough alone.

(b) Get really nervous and guilty, which results in you giving the ex your stereo and fridge.

(c) Borrow eight hundred dollars, say 'money walks', and never see them again.

If you answered (a) to these questions, there's some hope for you. You have potential but you need some tuition, so we recommend buying five or six copies of this book and placing them in every room of your house. Keep a copy with you at all times. And stop being so nice! The great thing about being a punster is that you can belittle people, slime those you want to bang, and still have them think you're a nice, intelligent, slightly eccentric person. So get cracking.

If you answered (b) to these questions, we suggest you go back to your room and have a Bex and a good lie down (be careful not to crease the jim jams your mother has laid out on the chenille bedspread). Get with the master plan! If you keep this up, you'll still be in the company of punsters, you'll just be the butt of all their jokes. We feel sorry for you, but only a little.

If you answered (c) to these questions, we're still trying to figure out why you took the test. You have got it! You show a devil-may-care attitude that is merely a gaudy façade for the explosive power of your intellect. This is the kind of book you could write, but you're probably too busy getting laid and having a great time at the best parties in town. Go forward and spread the Gospel according to Puns with our blessing.

BUGGERY

Buggers can't be choosers.

Arse and ye shall receive.

If you want to try something different,
go in one rear and out the other.

When Sherlock Holmes bent Watson over his desk and squeezed
some citrus over his butt, Watson wondered what he was up to.
Holmes replied: Lemon entry, my dear Watson.

Dinner party for sodomites: Bugger's Banquet.

Sodomites vows: to have and to hole.

The Rear of Living Dangerously.

Love cry: hole me tight!

Tush and shove.

CELLULITE

People who sell you stuff to get rid
of it have cottage cheese industries.

CHILDREN

Dinner with the kids: War and Peas.

You always herd the ones you love.

A boy hit his sister with a bowl of jelly and was charged with carrying a congealed weapon.

Too many sooks spoil the wrath.

A defenceless animal can be child's prey.

Babies don't have to do anything but lie there. That's why they're so nappy-go-lucky.

CO-DEPENDENCY

If you don't have the will power to leave the drug abuser you're living with, you have a junkie on your back.

CONDOMS

Gland in glove.

Cups and rubbers.

COOL

Cool people are scene and not herd.

CYNICS

A cynic is also called a Man About Frown.

CHILDREN AND PUNNING

'In the beginning was the pun.'
Samuel Beckett

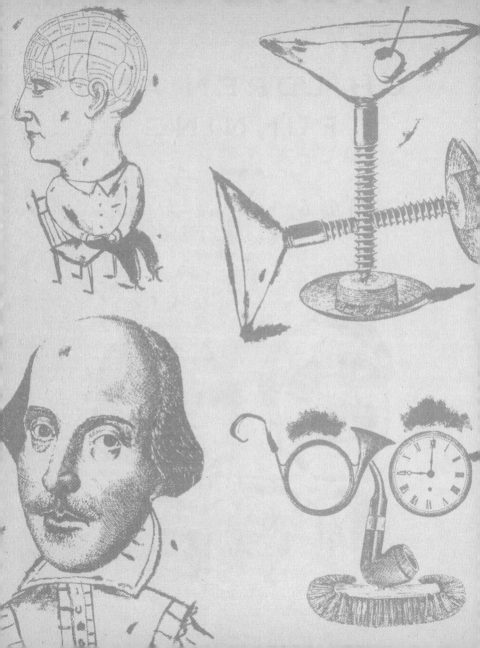

According to Don Anderson, '*Punster nascitur non fit.*' (A punster is born, not made.) We believe that, while some people seem to be more genetically predisposed to punning than others, *all* children are natural punsters. It's cultural and social conditioning that kills the urge to play with words, so that by the time a once-punster turns twenty-one, he can't lay down the most obvious *double entendre*. He has become 'civilised'.

The prime time to nurture punning in kids is at the very beginning when they start to make pre-verbal sounds. This is when language is most plastic. Though nonsense to outsiders, a parent's 'baby-talk' is profoundly effective in developing language skills in the infant. It's no coincidence that rhyming and sing-song are an essential part of this phase. When you recite, 'Little Jack *Horner* sat in a *corner* eating a Christmas pie …', it's not the information that's important, it's the music in the words. To make sense of the human sounds, babies need to order them—to hear similarities between words within repeating patterns. This is pre-punning terrain, and the child's hunger for linguistic tools makes him a perfect punning candidate.

Before children learn to read and they find out where one word stops and another begins, they have to play it by ear, so to speak. For instance, is it 'a nest' or 'an est'? I scream, you scream, we all scream for ice cream. We know a little girl who thought the singular form of 'clothes' was 'clo'. She was always asking to wear her favourite red clo. This is a wonderful stage in learning language because words are mutable, not set in stone or even type. Children imaginatively fill in the gaps in their linguistic body of knowledge because they have no choice. Necessity is the motor of invention. They make up words, often onomatopoeic ones. The dog is called 'Wuff' and the garden hose is a 'spish'. It makes sense to make a word sound like what it is or what it does. Or they will combine words, portmanteau style, because they don't know any better and it's an efficient way to get across their meaning. The more children make these 'mistakes', the more they master the language.

Often, they will create a pun within a half-known phrase. Like the three year old whose favourite game was 'hide and sneak'. This is an unintentional pun, but it shows how the mind naturally wants to order things by using a word similar to the 'real' word, only vaguely remembered, which still has some kind of contextual meaning. As soon as you tell children that they're wrong for coming up with an alternative solution and you give them the 'right' word, you inhibit them creatively and close off their punning valve. No wonder most grown-ups have trouble thinking laterally.

On the other hand, if you pun in front of them and encourage their punning instinct, you'll end up with happy, funny, well-adjusted kids who later in life will be invited to lots of dinner parties. They might even grow up to be master debaters or phenomenally overpaid talk-show hosts. Anything that empowers a child is good. Puns encourage the feeling of control, of being able to manipulate one of our most prized possessions.

So, even if you have to come up with a few puns in advance that you can drop into the conversation as if spontaneously, you should pun with your children. This can be particularly effective once the child is learning to read. You let them hear the potential of words while showing them the visual difference. Then they can play with puns like they do with mud or clay; you've got to let 'em get dirty. Since they're both aural and visual, puns have actual substance as well as conceptual life. Puns allow kids to stretch words and ideas as though they were elastic. Rhyming and word association games are a geat way to get the ball rolling, and kids love them.

Once you've given free rein to children's punnical proclivities, just watch them go. They'll pull words apart and put them back together like a doll or a truck. Vowels and consonants become linguistic Lego. They do what Victor Hugo called on us to do: '… mingle words, contaminate them, mix them up'. And even when punning is discouraged by parents and teachers afraid of the pun, kids will experiment. Like they will with sex and drugs a few years down the line. One of the first things they'll fool around with, if they haven't earlier, is each other's names at school. Ruby becomes 'Booby', Hugh becomes 'Huge', Jean is 'String Bean', Bob is 'Slob', Mulva is … Okay, you get the idea. The tendency is to make the kid sound stupid or gross in some way. If there's a chance to refer to poo or human genitalia, all the better.

So, like masturbation, punning in children should not be discouraged. The parent who comes down like a ton of bricks on a kid for saying 'fart' instead of 'foot' in some goofy context will regret his own squeamishness, especially when the kid later fails English and poetry because he was never allowed to have fun with words. Forcing a child not to pun goes against their nature as tricksters, mischief-makers.

Part of being a kid is to test limits. It's in the job description. They do it when they're telling a story about something that really happened, and they exaggerate the hell out of the details. 'I ate *three* ice blocks yesterday—no, actually I had *thirteen!*' They want to make the story as riveting as they can, and at the same time test the credibility threshold of their audience. Punning exercises the same faculties and satisfies them in the same way. Also, punning should be encouraged in children because it's a way to defy conventions and authority. You don't want a sheep for a kid, do you?

One of the most obvious ways children get into punning is through jokes. For most kids, the first joke they learn is a knock-knock joke or a riddle, both of which depend on puns. What's the favourite dessert in Australia? Boomeringue pie. What does an insect wear to bed? A gnat gown. What do grapes do when people step on them? They let out a little wine.

Your children probably already know a few, but if you want to steer them even further toward the road to punning pleasure, you can pass along the collection of pun jokes which follows.

PUN JOKES FOR JUNIORS

Q: Where are your buccaneers?
A: On your buccan'ead.

Q: What do rabbits do when they fall in love?
A: They live hoppily ever after.

Knock, knock.
Who's There?
Boo.
Boo who?
No need to cry—it's only a joke.

Q: What's a frog's favourite drink?
A: Croak-a-cola.

Q: What did the invisible boy call his mum and dad?
A: Transparents.

Q: Why did the little girl take a pencil to bed?
A: So she could draw the blinds.

Q: What do snakes do after a fight?
A: Hiss and make up.

Knock, knock.
Who's there?
Amos.
Amos who?
Amosquito.

Knock, knock.
Who's there?
Anna.
Anna who?
Anna 'nother mosquito.

A guy got a big increase in salary so he sent his dad on holiday.
He spent a week on the beach enjoying the son's raise.

Q: What do you call it when a crow gets laryngitis?
A: A lost caws.

Doctor: How did you get to my office so fast?
Patient: Flu.

Q: What do you call a blind dinosaur?
A: A d-ya-think-he-saurus.

Q: What do you call a blind dinosaur's dog?
A. A d-ya-think-he-saurus rex.

Girl: Should we order a salad?
Boy: Yes, lettuce.

Q: What flowers are under your nose?
A: Tulips.

An obstetrician makes her money on the stork market.

Knock, knock.
Who's there?
Banana.
Banana who?
Knock, knock.
Who's there?
Banana.
Banana who?
Knock, knock.
Who's there?
Banana.
Banana who?
Knock, knock.
Who's there?
Orange.
Orange who?
Orange ya glad I didn't say banana?

Q: What's the longest sentence in the world?
A: Life imprisonment.

Q: What kind of witches play cricket?
A: Wicket witches.

Tennis is such a noisy game. Players always raise a racket.

Q: What kind of boat does a shy sailor have?
A: A scared skiff.

Q: Where do burglars get their education?
A: In heist school.

Chef: I need some new kitchen knives.
Wife: I'll put them on my chopping list.

Q: What do you get when you pour boiling water down a button-hole?
A: Hot-cross-buttons.

Q: What does a nuclear scientist eat for lunch?
A: Fission chips.

Q: What do you call spiders who just got married?
A: Newlywebs.

Knock, knock.
Who's there?
Little Old Lady.
Little Old Lady who?
I didn't know you could yodel.

Q: What's a fish's favourite game?
A: Simple Salmon.

Q: What do you call a train with a dining car?
A: A chew-chew train.

Q: What do you call a woman who went off her diet?
A: A desserter.

The leopard almost escaped from the zoo, but was spotted.

Q: How did the cattle make life tough for the cowboy?
A: They played herd to get.

Q: What British magazine do ghosts read?
A: The Spooktator.

Woman: I'd like to buy a fur coat.
Salesperson: What fur?
Woman: Because it's freezing outside.

Cosmonauts speed into space—they're always Russian.

Knock, knock.
Who's there?
Isabella.
Isabella who?
Isabella necessary on a bicycle?

DATING

A guy's second-choice date: My Spare Lady.

Struggling to get off her bra: a storm in a D-cup.

Her date was foreign; he had Russian hands and Roman fingers.

When you go to a lingerie party you plan to pantie the town red.

If your date can change her behaviour skilfully she is Miss Demeanor.

If she jumps to conclusions she is Miss Construe.

If she's not mysterious she's Miss Understood.

If she has nice hair she's your Miss Tress.

If she hates her own gender she's Miss Ogynist.

If she's somebody else's she's Miss Taken.

If she steals your wallet she is Miss Appropriate.

If your bastard of a date is even worse than
the last one he is Mr Meaner.

Your first fight with a date is a baptism of ire.

If you can't pick up someone at the beach,
you must be dune something wrong.

Once you've finished an argument it's all over bar the pouting.

If you're dating a genie maybe you can get a massage in a bottle.

Her Italian date had a Roman nose—it was Roman all over his face.

A female deer chasing a speedy male deer:
a doe trying to mate a fast buck.

He thought he was her white knight,
but some other guy had his armour 'round her.

When you see one you want, go for bloke.

Someone who is captivated by another's scent is Smellbound.

If a guy's a jerk, tell him to get out of your bed and go home;
there's no rest for the dickhead.

Girl to obnoxious punster in pub: You're incorrigible.
Punster: So don't incorrige me.

Beware of geeks bearing gifts.

DEATH

A quiet undertaker is also known as the Hearse Whisperer.

If your parachute doesn't open it's known as jumping to a conclusion.

On hearing that the governor had commuted his death
sentence the prisoner declared: no noose is good news.

Dead men don't get laid.

DIETS

What you want to lose: The Shape of Fools.

Even if they work at first, you eventually put the weight
back on; the sleek shall inherit the girth.

You get so mad at excess weight, you're fat to be tied.

Clothes you can't fit into are to diet for.

When you can't lose weight around the tummy it's a midriff crisis.

Live and let diet.

Diets: They take your breadth away.

BABY WE WERE
BORN TO PUN

Even if They Deny It, Everybody Puns

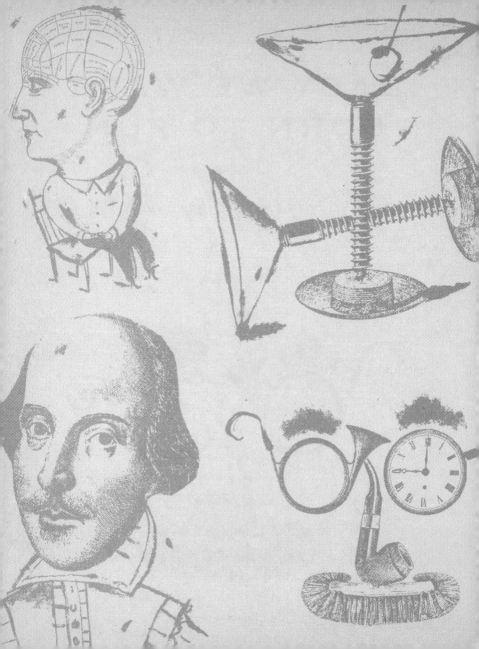

In *Les Miserables,* Victor Hugo writes, 'The most august, sublime and delightful examples of mankind, and perhaps beyond, have made plays on words. Jesus Christ made a pun on Peter, Moses on Isaac, Aeschylus on Polynices, Cleopatra on Octavian, and Spock on Kirk.' Actually that last one is ours. Just checking to see if you were awake. So, despite what the authorities would like you to believe, the best people do it, and it's as old as the hills.

Both Milton and Nietzsche associate punning with the devil. In *Paradise Lost,* Milton's pandemonium (literally, abode of all demons), is filled with violence and uproar—the sound of devils punning. It's a well-known fact that before the Fall, there was no such thing as ambiguity. There was only logic, order, clarity, and stainless steel. Nietzsche suggests that the first angel who punned was cast out of heaven, starting the whole ball rolling. After that, man's nature was split between good and evil, light and dark, not punning and punning. We find the latter much more interesting. The devil himself personifies a paradox. He is a bad angel. And a punster till hell freezes over.

The Assyrians and Babylonians were avid punsters. Sumerian was mainly written in ideograms, often with several meanings, or visual puns, like in modern Chinese. Ancient Sanskrit was permeated with puns. The beautiful Vedic hymns from the Hindu Rig-Veda are positively ablaze with puns. 'Agni' means fire, as well as specifically the sacrificial flame, and also 'the brilliant one', referring to god. So, three levels of meaning are folded into one word. Used in a similar way, puns are profuse and profound in Buddhist teaching. Indeed, the practice of meditation has been known to open the non-punster's mind to the joys of punning through the transcendence of linear thinking. Of course there are other good reasons to meditate, like spiritual fulfilment and stress management, but punning is a nice side-effect.

The ancient Greeks and Romans loved a good pun. Hermes/Mercury was the messenger of the gods but also the god of eloquence, wit and thieving. He was a trickster as well, with a split personality. Like the pun. In fact, we think we'd be pretty safe in appropriating Hermes/Mercury as the god of punning.

And speaking of gods, Jesus founded his church on a pun.

From Matthew VXI: 18: 'Thou art Peter [*Petros*] and upon this rock [*petra*] I will build my church.' A classic pun. Interesting to note that Peter himself may have misinterpreted the pun early on when he got petrified (from the Latin *petrificare*, Greek *petra*) and denied Jesus three times to save his own butt.

People pun in every known language on earth. Inuits, Italians, Lakota, Lithuanians, Mexicans, Malinese, Canadians and Kooris pun. The pun is considered to be one of the high points in traditional Japanese poetry, and puns abound in Hebrew—a trait which endures through Jewish punsters no matter what language they adopt. This exceptional phenomenon will be explored later.

The point is that punning is natural. A universal aspect of spoken and written language. As long as there are the same or similar words for different things, there will be puns. It's easy to find them; they're everywhere. In restaurants like Crêpe Expectations. The 'R' rated video shelves are downright tumescent with pun-titles like *On Golden Blonde, The Sperminator, Romancing the Bone, Crocodile Undie, Twat's New Pussycat,* and *Wetness for the Prosecution.*

A huge percentage of jokes and almost all riddles contain puns in their punchlines. What song do they play at a bent cop's wedding? Here comes the bribe. What kind of plane usually crashes? An error-plane. And a zillion others. Jokes with puns have been compared with unhealthy hair—oily at the roots and split at the ends. Often true. Limericks, especially the 'naughty' ones, are usually laced with puns, and puns appear regularly in crossword puzzles. Puns are invariably created when playing

Charades. You get to the pun through the visual clue which then leads you on to the secret phrase. In fact, good punsters are often good at Charades and other games like Nude Twister where exhibitionism and obscenity are considered a plus.

Being essentially subversive, puns are a common element in political satire under dictatorships and police states. Throughout World War II, the top-rated comic radio show in England was one based largely on puns, called 'ITMA' ('It's That Man Again'), the man being Hitler. The beauty is that fascists often don't get puns, their minds don't work that way. So, people can undermine censorship and taboos with a cleverly devised pun. You can utter a dirty word by not saying it exactly, but saying something similar.

RHYME AND PUNISHMENT

≈≈≈≈ or ≈≈≈≈

Is Punning a Sin?

Edgar Allen Poe said of puns that '... most dislike them who are least able to utter them'. Over the centuries, there have been moves to ban the pun, tax the pun and otherwise punish the pun. But, as Charles Lamb said, 'A pun is not bound by the laws which limit nicer wit.' Punsters don't like laws.

In something called *Everyman's Good English Guide*—just the title gives you the creeps—the pun is defined as 'a form of word-play traditionally received with a groan ... [it] is enjoyed by ordinary people (whose groans are usually feigned) but despised by the literary'. We guess they don't call Homer, Aeschylus, Virgil, Cicero, Chaucer, Shakespeare, Jonson, Hugo, Rabelais, Byron, Flaubert, Melville, Montaigne, Keats, Coleridge, Milton, Donne, Wordsworth, Wilde, Thoreau, Poe, Yeats, Joyce, Nabakov, Becket, Behan, Ionesco, Perelman, Orwell, Frost, Genet, and Pynchon 'literary'. Most writers pun, but every one of these punned profusely and in spite of the 'literary' establishment shunning the pun. But the word nazis don't get it. In one dictionary, the pun is defined as a 'form of wit, to which wise men stoop and fools aspire'. A handy turn of phrase, but horse shit as far as we're concerned. Arthur Koestler, who clearly couldn't tell the difference between write and wrong, said with a sneer that the pun is 'the most primitive form of human humour'. *Human* humour? What—like, as opposed to crustacean humour? Maybe in *his* hands it was primitive, but I guess he hadn't dipped into *Finnegans Wake* lately. Amoebe he should loosen up.

From the moment God flung the Devil out of paradise for punning, there has been a backlash against the pun. The righteous have always shit-canned it. Punning undermines the sanctity of words, and people who treat language as a sacred cow don't like this. We guess they think there's a lot at steak. They see the punster as the anti-Christ. Most self-proclaimed scholars in the fields of 'serious literature', philology, etymology, rhetoric and other boring farts disapprove of the pun. The pun is damned along with coinage, slang, foreign terms, mispronunciation, obscenity, incorrect spelling and 'bad' grammar—in short, most things that contribute to the evolution of language.

Some people reject punning because it's so accessible. You don't have to be rich or powerful or educated to do it. You don't even have to drive a fancy car. Puns are one of the most democratic aspects of language and snobs are threatened by this. People who look down on a pun act as if they never, even once, picked their nose. As H.W. Fowler in the *Dictionary of Modern English Usage* says, 'The assumption that puns are *per se* contemptible—betrayed by the habit of describing every pun … as *bad* … or … *feeble* … is a sign at once of sheepish docility and a desire to seem superior. Puns are good, bad and indifferent, and only those who lack the wit to make them are unaware of the fact.'

So, in spite of defenders like Fowler, punsters will never be universally loved. In fact, punning should come with a warning: 'Puns may make people hate you with a rare passion.' Many are simultaneously full of jealousy and loathing for the punster, for he is the dirty adventurer with the quick wit, the weird, musky smell and the world-weary good looks that can't be resisted. The backlash is inevitable.

BORN TO BE RILED

✦✦✦✦ or ✦✦✦✦

Mad About the Pun

Many so-called great men through history (women have once again stayed well away) have really let the pun piss them off. This discomfort is actually kind of fun to watch. The literary critic, Joseph Addison, commented at length on his own punniphobia in a 1711 issue of *The Spectator* in which he called punning '... false wit ... It is indeed impossible to kill a weed, which the soil has a natural disposition to produce. The seeds of punning are in the minds of all men [he makes it sound like a congenital disease]; and though they may be subdued by reason, reflection, and good sense, they will be very apt to shoot up in the greatest genius that is not broken and cultivated by the rules of art'. We like that phrase, '... genius that is not *broken* [our italics] ... by the rules of art'. That's the spirit, mister. *Break* that genius. Gee, if only Addison had been around to break Shakespeare with his rules of art ... Who makes up these rules of art, anyway? Always the wrong people—school prefects and former prison wardens. Addison goes on to write that he couldn't bear the pun, but he was all for 'being lashed with the manly strokes of wit and satire [now *that's* a revealing little metaphor]; for I am of the old philosopher's opinion, that if I must suffer from one or the other, I would rather it should be from the paw of a lion, than the hoof of an ass'. Not only is he being unrealistic (there being a lot more asses than lions about), but he demonstrates his virulently elitist attitude toward both his fellow man and wit in general. He and Joseph McCarthy would have loved each other. Book-burners of the world unite.

Some people don't like the fact that puns are immoderate. Critics have described the tendency to pun as punnitis, giving it decidely undeserved connotations. Puritanical types lump puns with sexual deviance and infanticide. They see punsters as perverts. And if they're happy to pervert the language, why not our morals, our children, indeed, religions and governments?! Puritans don't like the way puns break the rules. After all, puns show that words, like everything else in life, are unreliable. And like short skirts, beer, rock and roll and the race track, they have the power to corrupt. Puns are for people who are not afraid to embrace bad taste, the low life. Puns are for people who *get down*.

Voltaire was violently anti-pun, and spent a lot of time ranting and raving about this poisonousness little trick of wit. But who reads him anymore, anyway? Balzac agreed, and said that on a literary scale, the pun was of the same order as the comb and paper on the musical scale. Arthur Schopenhauer, master of the sour grape (sour gripe? sour grope? shower grope?), went out of his way to trash the pun as well. He obviously didn't have anything better to do, as he believed that the point of life was to renounce desire. Talk about uptight. Somebody give this guy a laxative.

These critics snubbed the pun for its apparent pointlessness. They never accepted the idea of the play instinct as a fundamental and positive human characteristic. Party poopers. So what if punning is unnecessary? It's the unnecessary stuff— like sex and chocolate—that makes life worth living.

Henri Bergson—the man with a forehead as big as his philosophical theory—was right about a lot of things but he couldn't accept the pun. He thought that *any* wordplay betrayed absentmindedness, even though it's obvious that the opposite is true. He actually called puns *slack*, when, if anything, they are hyperactive on several levels. Ah well, what do you expect from a guy who described life as a 'shell bursting into fragments which are again shells'. Sure it is.

Communications theorist Marshall McLuhan assailed the pun, but only as written: 'Simultaneities like puns and ambiguities—the life of spoken discourse—become, in writing, affronts to taste, floutings of efficiency.' We agree that the improvised pun which is a result of linguistic synchronicity has a special place in our puntheon, but to discard all written puns would be to lose some of the niftiest turns of phrase in all of literature. In the hands of a John Donne or a Thomas Pynchon, a pun imparts its secrets gradually as the multiple levels of meaning emerge on careful reading and re-reading, like a literary dance of the seven veils. In print, the emotional dynamic of a pun is different from its conversational counterpart. McLuhan's most famous quote is 'The medium is the message' which someone later rephrased in a pun, 'The medium is the massage.' The latter may be even more to the point, so lighten up, Marshall.

Ultimately, one can't deny that jealousy may be a factor in

these attacks. We mean, neither Voltaire nor Schopenhauer were famous for their sense of humour, and everybody knows that the funny guys are the ones who get laid. As Jack Benny said, echoing Edgar Allan Poe's inescapable truth: 'The only reason people complain about puns is that they never thought of them first.'

And some folks put down the pun even though they're great punsters themselves! They believe they should stop, but they can't. Many seek counselling. It's like drinking, gambling, smoking, cross-dressing, sleeping with your boss's spouse and everything else that's fun. Sometimes you just can't help yourself. There's probably a twelve-step program for punsters anonymous. A typical sufferer was Oliver Wendell Holmes who called punning 'Verbicide—violent treatment of a word with fatal results to its legitimate meaning.' Of course in that quote he coins a portmanteau and reveals the sorry truth: he was an incurable pun junkie. A man divided against himself. In the end he lost the duel with duality and died a shameful punster.

One nineteenth century self-doubter, Sydney Smith, said, 'Puns … are in very bad repute, and so they ought to be. The wit of language is so miserably inferior to the wit of ideas, that it is very deservedly driven out of good company.' Exactly. Bad company is much more fun. He went on, 'Sometimes, indeed, a pun makes its appearance which seems for a moment to redeem its species; but we must not be deceived by them; it is a radically bad race of wit.' Ironically, this man was such a severe punaholic, he would have given away his first born for the chance to slip in the odd pun. There is some evidence that he did. He was like Dr

Jekyll and Mr Hyde, the latter being the hairy-palmed punster whom he could not control until he killed him, and himself.

Punsters who fight their true nature rarely succeed for long. Even a small amount of alcohol has been known to melt the resolve of the staunchest anti-pun crusader. Rabelais was like this, and probably suffered from alcohol-and-pun-induced blackouts, as he would pun shamelessly in company then later deny his own quips. He loved to condemn punning, but punned daily. Maybe he thought it was easier to get away with if he pretended to be on the side of righteousness and linguistic purity. Or perhaps he simply accepted the paradox of the pun, best exhibited by Fred Allen when he said, 'Hanging is too good for a man who makes puns; he should be drawn and quoted.'

To small-minded, linear thinkers, the pun is a solecism—a sin against grammar, as well as just plain bad manners. Too bad—they go through life missing the freedom and poetry of the pun. Even the *Encyclopaedia Britannica* seemed to catch on in its attempt to explain why some people sink so low: 'It may be that [the pun] is a means whereby individuality is expressed, due order and the rational are subverted, and personal independence asserted …' Precisely. The revolutionary Soviet filmmaker, Sergei Eisenstein (a ground-breaking visual punster) described puns as verbal montage. He suggested that the juxtaposition of mental images conjured up by the punster creates an emotional reaction in the listener. Punavision. Precisely what movies do, but puns manage it for a fraction of the cost and without the interference of an executive producer.

Samuel Taylor Coleridge, who was on opium at the time, put
it a little differently: '... words are not mere symbols of things and
thoughts but themselves things, and ... any harmony in the
things symbolised will perforce be presented to us more easily as
well as with additional beauty, by a correspondent harmony of
the symbols with each other'. So, contrary to what some might
claim, punsters actually treat words with more respect than the
non-punner by endowing them with more intrinsic power.

Several commentators have suggested that the test of real wit
is whether or not it is still there if translated into another language. This is an absurd measure of wit, as it invalidates *all* wordplay and indeed all poetry whose rhyme and rhythm are lost in
exact translations.

So the hell with the word nazis. We'll just take Anthony
Burgess's advice and let sleeping dogmas lie.

THE EVIL TWIN

⚜ or ⚜

The Bad Pun

In this book, there are actually two questions we need to answer. The first is: is it bad to pun? As we have already explained, no, it is not; punsters perform a vital service to the community. But the second question is, are there bad puns? And of course the answer is a resounding yes!

Many rubbishers of the pun are probably so disgusted with all the really dreadful puns around that they reject the lot for being innately bad form. The excruciating ones that creak and groan with bleeding obviousness or sheer meaninglessness give the clever ones a bad name. Good puns have been found guilty by association for centuries. Charles Lamb was referring to all puns but we think his words apply particularly well to the bad pun: 'A pun … is a pistol let off at the ear; not a feather to tickle the intellect.'

Another problem is that some punsters claim that the worst puns are the best. We reject this trite contradiction for being lazy and ignorant. That infamous punbroker, Bennett Cerf, actually collected horrible, simplistic puns in several books. One, from *Bennett Cerf's Treasury of Atrocious Puns,* typifies the rest: 'Q: What's a crick? A: The noise made by a Japanese camera.' The sort of adult who is delighted by this gag also enjoys waiting for water to boil and watching *The Ricky Lake Show.* We know, we know, who's the snob now—but we've got to draw the line somewhere. Some puns are even worse, if you can believe it, and probably shouldn't be called puns. They're the ones that capitalise on words' similar sounds without any corresponding connection through meaning. For example: You can pay for the eggs but the Amazon me. Now, ham and eggs and Amazon don't have any connection within the context of the joke. It's not a play on words in their full sense, merely a play on sounds—ham-is-on, and Amazon. So it's a bad pun, if a pun at all. In contrast: a gypsy needs lots of roam. It may be a lame pun, but at least a valid nexus of meaning emerges from the use of the word roam instead of room.

Like eating perfectly cooked chips or those peanuts they give you on airplanes, once you start punning, you can't stop. When a punster turns on the punning switch in his brain and gets a head of steam going, he will hear all conversation through a punning filter. This paranomania can become very tedious. Bystanders/ victims feel like boxers in the fifteenth round—they just want to throw in the vowel. The punner will sometimes spew out puns indiscriminately until he falls asleep or is bludgeoned to death by friends. But not before some desperately hideous puns have escaped his throat.

Freud studied the psychology of wit in depth, and recognised this phenomenon of compulsive punning. He wrote that 'There are some people who, when they are in high spirits, can, for considerable periods of time, answer every remark addressed to them with a pun.' But his conclusion after observing this mania is important to note.

He thought the quality of the puns deteriorated progressively during these punning fits, not necessarily because the punster had run out of good puns, but because he may have been influenced by the contempt with which his puns were regarded. In other words, the more the punner drove everyone crazy, the more they assaulted him and the worse his puns became. Paranomaniacs of this calibre are to be handled with extreme care and will be discussed later.

DRIVING

The fastest prime mover on the road is the Star Truck.

A nervous driver is the Road Worrier.

The Harley Davidson manual is called *As You Bike It*.

In Mexico, when your engine conks out it might be your car burrito.

When the cop pulled over a truckie with a simliar rego as the guy he was looking for he said, 'Lorry, wrong number.'

The prime mover matriarch is a mother-trucker.

DRUGS

The guy who works in the national park up near Byron is called The Stoned Ranger.

Coke dealer: the Lizard of Schnozz.

On quaaludes your partner is party in your hands.

Give me Librium or Give me Meth.

Needle sharing: Dangers On A Vein.

Smoking joints is all give and toke.

Junkie's lament: I'm stingin' in the vein.

When you're stoned blind it's bong time no see.

Where there's coke there's ire.

If it's the kind of grass that makes you horny,
then sex marks the pot.

DUTY

Duty's only sin deep.

EMERGENCIES

Sometimes the situation is too dire for!

When you get mugged by a guy who can't even count
the money in your wallet, that's a dolt hood.

EMPLOYMENT

The polite usher said, 'Pleased to seat you.'

Cleaners know that grime doesn't pay.

Bakers don't get paid enough; they knead more dough.

A cleaner is a mould digger.

What you get if you're a coal miner: grime and punishment.

A decade as a cleaner is ten years tied to the must.

Compulsive sound recordist: I never met a man I didn't mike.

The real estate agent has a vista'd interest in the property.

Mouldy ship's cook's lament: how green was my galley.

Flabby, unsuccessful waiter: loose hips sink tips.

The guy digging for coal finally quit because
he was bored out of his mine.

The cleaner had a heart of mould.

Builders sometimes take amphetamines to increase
productivity; it's life in the fast crane.

Slack photographer to client: someday your prints will come.

The brother car restorers: partners in chrome.

A job cleaning bathrooms is worth its weight in mould.

A discovered assassin: the spied sniper.

THE JUNG AND
THE RESTLESS

The Psychology of the Pun

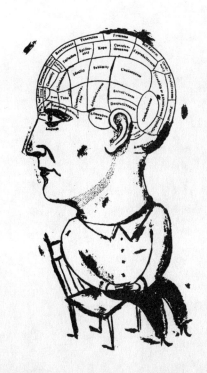

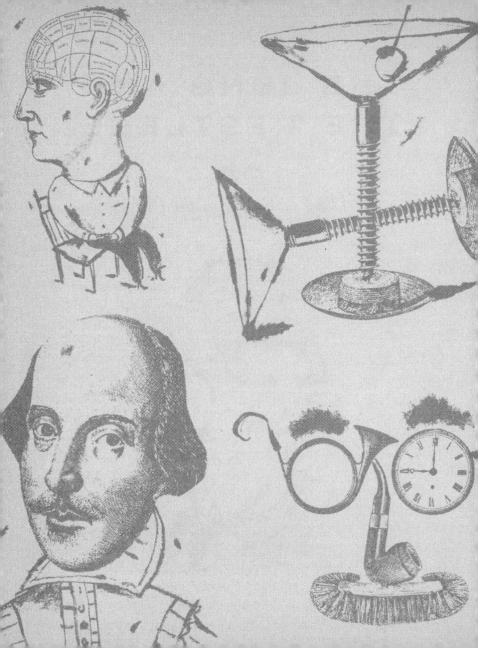

In addition to all his political shit-kicking, Noam Chomsky transformed the study of linguistics with a ground-breaking psychological theory. Philosophers and scientists had been suggesting the same thing for a long time, but Noam pulled it all together in his brand of psycholinguistics. Basically, he said that every phrase we utter is a map to psychic systems that are hard-wired into the brain from birth. The way we use language is a genetically determined skill, like personal waste disposal. No matter what schools we went to, all of us use grammatical structures which we didn't have to learn. In other words, language isn't as much an act of intellect as one of instinct. Punning is one of the acts which reveals the fundamental structure of language. Mind over patter.

Psychologists have long recognised the importance of the play instinct in human behaviour, of which wordplay is an indispensable aspect. Like craving cheeseburgers and having sex, playing with language is programmed into us. The impulse is innate. Inexorable. The mind naturally likes to associate, order things through sound, shape and meaning. That's how we learn. Punning is a playful verbal demonstration of association. So no matter what the social or cultural environment, punning is bound to occur.

Biological necessity governs the structure and use of language, as it does a lot of things, like the way we're organised socially. We use language the way we do because of the special characteristics of our species. It's hard to say exactly which physical or biological characteristics created the urge to pun, but there are theories. Some say the urge begins in the groin and is then channelled through the liver which gives orders to the brain. Others have suggested that the source is the elbow, which is occasionally used to drive home the point of a pun, particularly a bad one. Others believe that the lips are far too interesting to have been designed just for whistling and must have had something to do with early pun formation, but we personally believe that kissing came before whistling *or* making puns and is more important than either. It *is* true that although dolphins have a sophisticated language, they probably don't pun, and in fact have neither elbows nor lips, so there may be something to both theories. And if you *do* find a punning dolphin, call David Letterman now.

THE SHADOW KNOWS

or

Where in Your Head Puns Come From

Psychologists have always recognised that punning has its place and is an expression of our hidden feelings. Freud believed that the main purpose of wordplay was to create a safe outlet for repressed impulses. Perhaps this is why puns are so often about sex. We pun not just to disguise lewd meaning from the censors, but because puns are a natural siphon for thoughts about sex. On a deep level, they're closely connected; sex and wit have always gone gland-in-hand. Everyone wants a partner who's really funny *and* a great lover, although not necessarily at the same time. If you look at 'personals' ads, you'll notice that a sense of humour is at least as important as good looks and the absence of a criminal record.

There are two kinds of puns—intentional and unintentional, and in Jungian terms there is an archetype for each of them. The intentional, or conscious pun, comes from the Trickster in us. The Trickster represents the first, least evolved stage in the hero myth. The Trickster's behaviour is instinctual, uninhibited, childish. Koestler calls it merely infantile, but (luckily for him) associates it with intuition which leads to invention. The Trickster's physical appetites dominate his behaviour and he has all the social graces of a two year old at dinnertime. He can often be cruel, and always mischievous. Sounds like the punsters you know, doesn't it? We don't have to be dominated by the Trickster in us to pun, we just need to let him take over temporarily, when the urge is undeniable. People ruled by their Trickster often become serial punsters, whom we will investigate shortly.

The unintentional pun corresponds to the Shadow, and like his step-brother, the Trickster, he is not civilised and rarely knows how to act. The Shadow represents everything in us of which we are unconscious. (Spooner's shadow must have had him in a stranglehold.) Because we repress a lot of what we think is bad in us which ends up bouncing around inside the walls of our unconscious looking for a way out, the Shadow has come to be inaccurately perceived as our dark or negative side. Not necessarily. The Shadow comprises things like our so-called animal instincts. When we make an unintentional pun, it's often our Shadow stepping out from our unconscious into the cold light of day. Usually to our great embarrassment. In other words, the Shadow-inspired unintentional pun reveals what we are *really* thinking about. Another word for this is the parapraxis, better known as the Freudian slip.

Freud recognised that when people commit a slip of the tongue, it is never completely innocent. Often, when someone uses a word that sounds something like the word they *meant* to use, creating a pun, the accidental replacement indicates a wish or conflict within the unconscious. We've all done it and denied what it implies about what's going on inside our sordid little minds, but a sharp shrink could bust us in seconds flat then make us pay for the honour. And that's exactly what Carl Jung did when using a word association game with one of his patients. Several times, the patient made Freudian slips which suggested to Jung that the guy had committed a murder. After being confronted with the testimony of his own unconscious by the crafty analyst, the patient confessed his crime. Later, the judge threw the book at him, insisting that 'No pun intended' was an insufficient defence.

One of our favourite Freudian slips was perpetrated by the headmaster of Diana Dors' high school. Usually cast in the role of a good-time girl in her films of the 1940s, Diana's original surname was Fluck, which she wisely gave the flick. Before a class reunion, the headmaster was terrified he would make a mistake and utter an obscenity when he introduced her to the assembly, so he rehearsed her real name dozens of times ... Diana *Fluck* ... Diana *Fluck* ... Diana *Fluck*. When the time came, he was perfectly composed and didn't stumble for a moment when he announced, 'And now, I know you all want to give a big welcome to our best known alumna, Diana Clunt.'

Because Tricksters and Shadows are pretty slippery customers, a lot of people try not to give them any airtime. Confronted with their own expression of these archetypes, most people can feel, as James Joyce said, 'like children—Jung and easily Freudened'. They're afraid they'll never get invited to another dinner party if they let those puns loose. That may or may not be the case depending on the circles you move in, but it's dangerous to deny these aspects of yourself. Pun-suppression can lead to terrible mental and physical health problems which can take years of therapy and expensive medication to undo. There is anecdotal evidence that lower backache, chronic fatigue syndrome, adrenal exhaustion and bleeding gums have all been brought on by gagging the pun.

Most psychologists agree that in moderation, it is important to pun. For Freud, punning, as with all humour, was a triumph of the ego. Puns make us conscious that we are using language—an activity that most of us perform without thinking. To some, consciousness is an intrusion. To others, it's a tool which liberates and gives pleasure. Punning displays the ability to think laterally, literally and littorally at the same time. It's one of the things that sets us apart from the squid.

PHALLUS IN WONDERLAND

or

Punning ... in Your Dreams

There is one place that we pun freely, without the constraints of culture or the influence of chemicals, and that is in our dreams. All we have to do is look. The unconscious aspects of events, things and people are revealed to us in our dreams through symbols. These symbols can be in the form of images, words, or actions, and often their meaning becomes apparent when we realise they are actually puns. As Anthony Burgess explains, 'In *Alice in Wonderland* ... A school of fishes becomes a real school by the dream-law which takes homonymous puns not as jokes but as statements of double fact, and all that follows has to confirm the duality.' Burgess's example is a visual pun, but we often dream in verbal puns as well.

A friend of ours has a recurring dream that she is trying to get to Seoul, South Korea, a place she has never been and to which she has no connection. Sometimes she is staring at the board at the airport, checking the departure time for the flight bound for Seoul. Other times, she is on her way to Seoul, happily winging through the clouds to this ultimate destination. We don't think we need to pay anybody $75 an hour to tell us that she's really dreaming about finding her soul. When another friend had a recent professional breakthrough, she felt that she was starting a new life. She dreamt that she gave birth, painlessly, to a baby girl and called her Esme. Clearly, Esme really meant 'is me', and the baby was herself, reborn. A male friend had a dream that his wife accused him of not driving safely with the children in the car. He kept shouting at her, 'That's a fallacy! A bald-faced fallacy!' It turns out that the guy had been having an affair and felt guilty about it. In his dream he was admitting that his wrong-doing had nothing to do with his driving; it was his phallus—his *bald-faced* phallus—that was putting his family in jeopardy.

Many writers have recognised and played with the link between puns and dreams in their work. As Freud said, both puns and dreams use 'faulty reasoning, absurdity, indirect representation, representation by the opposite'. In *Alice in Wonderland*, Lewis Carroll uses both visual and verbal puns to tell the story of Alice's unconscious. Wonderland is her dream, and just about everything in it is punnically symbolic. James Joyce explores similar territory in *Finnegans Wake* which we'll attempt to explore later. Believe it or not.

A MIND LIKE A SPIV

 or

The Pathology of Punning

It is said that language is a mirror of the mind, and in some pun-sters' case, cracked ones. Even the most innocent-seeming joke may be symptomatic of mental instability. Freud said that humour can indicate a pathological state: '… the subjective determinants of the joke-work are often not far removed from those of neurotic illness'. A pun, like certain forms of insanity, can have an internal logic which does not apply in the 'real' world. R.D. Laing might have theorised that punning is a sane man's reaction to an insane world. In any case, think twice about moving in with a heavy punster, and *never* leave him alone with your children.

Some psychologists have observed that punning can be a form of passive aggression. Within a socially acceptable framework— the apparently innocent play on words—there can be a subtle but implicit insult. After all, the punster undermines the other per-son's word or phrase by making light of it. And he devalues not only their words but their ideas and point of view. We mentioned this earlier as a selling point, but of course, if the puns are indis-criminate, the punster is probably neurotic. An example of this is the character of Hamlet. In Shakespeare's tragedy the hero spouts puns left and right, often to belittle the character he's talking to in the name of dramatic irony. Part of the time, Hamlet is merely pretending to be mad and he uses puns and wordplay to reinforce this perception. At other times it seems he's really coming apart at the seams, and his endless puns are symptoms of true madness.

The accepted psychological wisdom seems to be that heavy punsters suffer from deep-seated insecurities. Perhaps it's as simple as the Class Clown Syndrome which springs from a need for attention and acceptance. Perpetual punning is a good way to distract one's peers from perceived shortcomings like body odour, obesity and advanced leprosy, as it can continually interrupt or deflect lines of inquiry. In other words, punning can be a decoy. Other theories suggest that those who pun simply fear being taken seriously. No matter what the tone of the conversation, a punster can nudge it away from the solemn and sober with the unbearable lightness of punning. Some experts have seriously suggested that compulsive punning is symptomatic of pathological states possibly including impotence. Some believe that puns are motivated by revenge and can get very nasty. We don't know whether or not punning is big in Sicily, but we're interested in any evidence.

Like any obsessive-compulsive type, the out-of-control punster will cling to his habit even after he's lost his job, his family, and the respect of his neighbours. And he has no *self*-respect, but he doesn't care. Only the pun matters. In describing Shakespeare's obsession with the pun, Dr Johnson could be talking about an addict and his smack habit: 'A quibble [pun], poor and barren as it is, gave him such delight, that he was content to purchase it, by the sacrifice of reason, propriety, and truth. A quibble was to him that fatal Cleopatra for which he lost the world, and was content to lose it.' We dare you to find a better description of a junkie.

But even the bard was outdone in the playwright-as-pun-addict-stakes by the Marquis de Bièvre, a Frenchman who was a compulsive punner. He actually wrote a play called *Vercingentorixe* which had a pun in every single line. Even the French didn't let him get away with that crap, and the play has never been performed at the risk of inducing mass suicide.

Psychotics often invent bizarre words. Of course, so do academics, politicians and sports commentators. But obsessive wordplay and punning has always been recognised as being more common among the mentally disturbed. As Eastman said in his book about humour, 'There are forms of insanity in which ... a "flight of ideas" occurs, which is like the racing of a motor disgeared from the machine it was intended to move, and in this condition puns are sometimes seen to fly off in the most extraordinary swarms and galaxies.' We're going crazy just reading about it.

Schizophrenics are sometimes known to pun when they confuse form and substance. They might see the word as the thing more than the idea it represents. But theirs are unintentional puns. Their linguistic confusion is involuntary and not meant for an audience. In fact, schizophrenics often don't understand jokes, because ironically, they can't get the double meaning.

One *Dictionary of Speech Pathology* describes punning as a form of embolophrasia—one of the symptoms being a pathological play on words of the same sound with a different meaning. This apparently can be found in the manic stage of manic-depressive psychosis. We hate when that happens.

In *Stedman's Medical Dictionary*, this disease was given another name which has a really nice ring to it. It's called 'Witzelsucht', which is 'a morbid tendency to pun … while being oneself inordinately entertained thereby'. Back in the 1920s they thought Witzelsucht, also called 'Förster's Syndrome', might be associated with frontal lobe tumours. So they yanked a few frontal lobes out, just in case. Thank God they didn't get to Groucho Marx.

Of course, tumours turned out not to be the problem, although it has been observed that in improvised jazz and spontaneous punning we access the same part of the brain they remove in a lobotomy. So the connection may yet be made. A chemical imbalance may also contribute to uncontrolled punning, but so far no drug has been found to correct it. On the contrary, drugs just seem to encourage the worst impulses in the pathological punster. Scientists are working to isolate the punning gene, which, if found, could be engineered to shut down in polite society. Some people are amused by the compulsive punster, and after he's gone, they're still laughing until they realise their wallet is missing.

These days, most psychologists believe that compulsive punning is simply an unconscious reaction to mental disintegration. That *is* good news.

PORTRAIT OF A SERIAL PUNSTER

꧁ or ꧁

Punning Out of Control

Like the serial killer, the serial punster has a very particular *modus operandi*. The order in which he (in spite of the leaps forward made by women in the last quarter century, female serial punsters are still virtually unknown) carries out the selection of his victims as well as the sequence of consequent puns are critical features. Once a serial punster has subdued his victim, he will often tie them to a piece of furniture and pun continuously until the victim goes mad, begging to be killed before being hit with another pun. But when not in the act of committing their crime, serial punsters aren't obviously insane. They move among us with relative ease because they have learned to control their punning. Some of them are loners, but some appear to be happily married, with 2.2 kids and a house in the 'burbs. Many even hold down steady jobs, often in the service industries, journalism, or publishing. They know that if they gave free rein to their thirst for punnilingus, they would be cast out of society and denied employment. But most of them live on the edge and like it there.

These days, they don't usually lock up serial punsters or take out their frontal lobes. For better or worse, the civil rights of people who choose to pun at will are protected by law. But there are ways to recognise the natural born punster, and forewarned is forearmed. A list of attributes which typify the serial punster follows; some may be afflicted with all or only some of these traits. If they seem to describe someone you know, gently suggest some form of therapy, or just move to Irian Jaya and get an unlisted phone number.

—usually male, over twenty-one years of age
—moody, emotional
—aggressive
—obsessed with bodily functions
—drinks, uses drugs
—sexually voracious, often kinky
—rebellious
—intelligent
—funny
—exhibitionist
—large head (could be his brain, could be a tumour)
—large hands
—large vocabulary
—pulls the wings off flies
—has no respect for authority
—hogs crossword puzzles, watches 'Ren & Stimpy'

Come to think of it, this guy sounds perfect.

EXERCISE

Lycra or lump it.

FAMILY

Her father was Spanish and her mother was Jewish,
so she didn't know if she was Carmen or Cohen.

Patriarchal clan: you could knock me down with a father.

From a baby's point of view, Mummy makes the world go around.

The family with a lot of convictions is full of bros and cons.

Nicholas of Russia's mum's first words to him: a tsar is born.

Björk's mum's first words to her: a star is björn.

When she's living on the street, drooling a lot,
you call her your vaguer aunt.

The Lion King is the father of the pride.

Queen Elizabeth with her daughters-in-law: the Lady banishes.

FARMING

A chicken farmer is also known as an eggistentialist.

A farmer who's had enough feels that he's been there, dung that.

The drought-stricken farm is always doing its lawn dry.

When the grass gets too long, the farmer believes that less is mow.

Farmers: natural born tillers.

She was only the farmer's daughter but all the horse manure.

His wife left him, but the farmer tractor down.

The farmer who was crushed in a sheep stampede died in the wool.

When a few drops of rain fall in the middle of a long drought, the
farmer says, 'Moisture do about nothing.'

The farmer's channel: Hay TV.

When the sheep won't shut up, the bleat goes on.

Farmers like to get to the point when discussing erosion—
what it all soils brown to.

FASHION

Style slaves are absolutely fatuous.

Flabbery will get you no wear.

The company run by logical fabric-makers is called Rational Velvet.

The chic shall inherit the flirt.

The designer's biography was called *The Rayon,
the Bitch and the Wardrobe*.

Comment on the model in mohair: what a hair-suit young man.

Backstage near the catwalk: from rags to bitches.

She looked great in her black leather pants—her dominant jeans.

Models with a lot of goo in their hair are Gel's Angels.

Leather pants left to dry on the line will end up as withering hides.

Cricketers are the only ones who still like upper-lip facial hair and
think the mo', the merrier.

With tight-fitting lingerie the woman says,
'The suspender is killing me.'

Someone who finally comes around to synthetic
fashion is better latex than never.

Pete Townshend: The Modfather.

Buying only things on sale from the shopping complex:
mall's well that spends well.

Her dresswear lingerie that reveals more than she means to is her
Freudian slip.

Haute couture is often tongue-in-chic.

Mini-skirts are in; it's good to keep your thighs peeled.

FINANCE

Uranium sales: profit of doom.

A product that doesn't sell despite a
big ad campaign goes against hype.

With your first coup on the stock market you get a taste of money.

Part of the movie *Babe*'s profit,
and maybe the name of the sequel: Pig Million.

The insurance assessor can't take things on fake value.

They guy won millions but it still didn't buy him happiness. He said,
'Lotto good it did me.'

THE PUN IS MIGHTIER THAN THE SWORD

A Literary Pack of Punsters

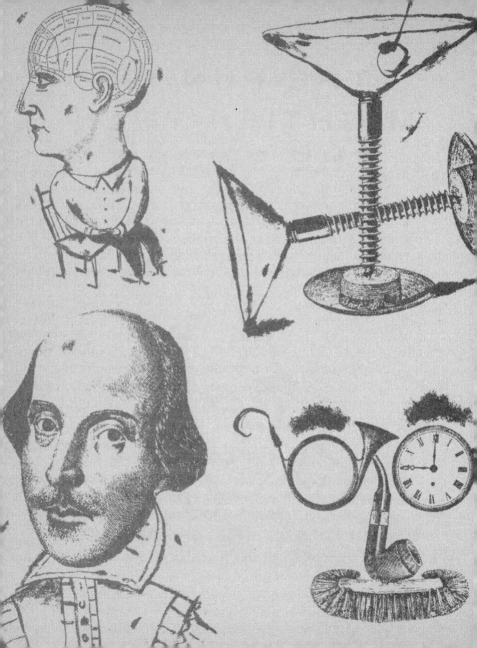

 As we mentioned earlier, many people cling to the belief that classy writers don't debase themselves by employing the pun. As Freud put it, 'The Paranomasia, or Pun, is well known in ordinary conversation, and in comic writing, but rarely enters into serious composition.' To put it simply, this is a heap of steaming cow shit.

Arguably the greatest writers and thinkers in history used the humble paranomasia. Socrates punned, as did Plato, under his tutelage. Along with stuff like irony and logic, the pun was a valued weapon in their rhetorical arsenal. And although he later rejected Plato's philosophy in favour of science, Aristotle concurred with his teacher on the use of the pun, saying that paragrams were among the beauties of good writing.

The Greek playwrights including Aeschylus, Sophocles and Euripides were avid punsters—as avid as Ovid and the rest of the the Romans, including Juvenal, Lucretius and Virgil. Like the Greeks, they often used puns to refer to down-to-earth aspects of everyday life such as dildos, shitting, farting, incest and pederasty. The ambiguity of the pun let them approach these subjects from a suitably oblique angle. Cicero was the most devoted Roman punster. He not only punned in his writing, but recommended use of the pun in his rules of oratory. So brush up on your Latin and you're in for a real treat. (We haven't included any of the Greek or Roman puns because they tend to lose something in the translation. Not that we don't know Latin and Greek.) Anyway, Cicero's puns flowed naturally, whereas Virgil's were more forced. In fact, they were sometimes absurdly contrived. This was Virgil on the ridiculous.

Although punning continued to occur unchecked all over the world as languages evolved, things were quiet on the Western font for quite a while after the Romans. Except for Chaucer, it wasn't until those hard partyers, the Elizabethans, got going that the literary punsters got back into action. That's when the Big Daddy of all literary punsters was born, and we will give William Shakespeare his own chapter a bit later.

Shakespeare and fellow punsmiths like Christopher Marlowe and Ben Jonson used the quibble to such great effect that in the early seventeenth century, during the reign of King James I, the pun experienced perhaps its most exalted status in history. James adored the pun and surrounded himself with a constant party of punsters. He actually went as far as to reward serial punsters with high positions at court or in the church. Seriously. This gave the pun even more credibility than it had under Elizabeth. Suddenly, it was not only cool to pun, it was the aristocratic thing to do. There were, as always, humorous puns, but increasingly puns were used in tragedies for dramatic ironic effect. Even religious literature and teaching were laced with puns. People punned openly in the streets.

And if you're looking for punning in the best of the metaphysical poets, consider it Donne. John Donne exploded the construct of the Elizabethan sonnet to create a poetry dense with offbeat imagery and obscure references to art, science and crafts through the use of fractured metre, syntax and guess what—the pun. In *Hymn to God the Father* he has a bit of fun with his own name:

> When thou hast done, thou has not done.
> For I have more …
> I have a sin of fear, that when I have spun
> My last thread, I shall perish on the shore;
> But Swear by Thy self, that at my death Thy Son
> Shall shine as he shines now, and heretofore;
> And having done that, Thou hast done;
> fear no more.

Not only is there all that done/Donne punning, but 'Son'

means both Christ and 'sun'. In *The Canonization,* he waxes poetic about orgasm and erection as *le petit mort* when he puns, 'wee dye and rise the same'. Being a real verbal gymnast, many of Donne's puns are hard to get, but profoundly satisfying once you do.

In his earlier noted attack on the pun, Joseph Addison claimed that Cambridge University was at one time 'infested with Puns; but whether or no this might arise from the fens and marshes in which it was situated, and which are now drained, I must leave to the determination of more skilful naturalists.' Himself a graduate of Oxford, Addison was probably thinking of John Milton when he assailed Cambridge for its punfestation. A Cambridge-trained scholar and poet, Milton was—unusually for a punster—a Puritan. But it's important to understand that his puns are made in the spirit of revolt, in this case, against the Church of England. In his epic poem, *Paradise Lost,* Milton presents his theological vision while punning his way to hell and back.

Thousands of puns have been identified in Milton's work. Many are obvious and clearly intentional, many are probably unconscious (especially given his puritanical repression of certain topics). By the modern reader, many will be missed or misunderstood, because so many of the meanings of words are archaic. A large percentage of his puns recall Latin, Greek and Hebrew derivations, so unless you're up on your classic lingos, you'll be in lingo limbo. But *Paradise Lost* is still worth a read, if only for the encounters with Satan. Among Milton's devils, punning was an expression of excess and abuse. Satan himself puns grotesquely, shamelessly, and rallies other angels with his nasty puns. So forget all that stuff about Eve and the apple. Satan's pun was the Original Sin. Some anti-pun critics excuse Milton for these wicked puns because he was only trying to characterise the demons as guilty of the worst kind of behaviour. But Jesus also puns in *Paradise Lost*, although less profusely, and virtually all of Milton's work is distinguished by the odd paragram. It has also been suggested that some of Milton's puns were typos. Apparently, the guy was blind, and dictated his work to people who might not have had his spelling ability. In addition, printers weren't known for their assiduous proofreading, and of course there's the possibility that a serial punster might have transcribed his poetry or worked at the printer, sabotaging the work of the most celebrated English poet after Shakespeare with cheap puns. Yeah, right.

Alexander Pope had a killer wit, and used puns to express his basically bitter and twisted take on life in his satires. We suspect that the pun-as-a-decoy phenomenon, combined with the Class Clown Syndrome may have been at work, as poor Pope was all of 148cm tall and a hunchback to boot.

In *Gulliver's Travels*, Jonathan Swift was a dedicated follower of his punning instincts, to the point where language, rather than meaning, sometimes drives the tale. He had that in common with Shakespeare, Thoreau and James Joyce, as he did their scatalogical concerns, often in pun-form. Great minds stink alike.

During the Restoration, in the latter part of the seventeenth and into the eighteenth centuries, there was a backlash against the pun. Good things never last. Puns were actually banned from journalism, 'serious' literature and sermons, and were only tolerated in strictly defined comedies. Punsters were lumped together with carriers of the plague and would-be revolutionaries and, like many of the latter, went underground. It was a dark time for the literary pun.

Like Prohibition, the ban eventually gave way to a groundswell of public pressure, and punning re-emerged as an acceptable form of wit in the nineteenth century. John Keats, that sensuous Romantic poet who was also a master of his craft, had a soft spot for the pun. He called sentences with puns 'ten senses'. But his love of wordplay increased pathologically, so that as he neared death from tuberculosis he wrote: 'I have an habitual feeling of my real life having past, and that I am leading a posthumous existence ... Yet I ride the little horse and, at my worst, even in Quarantine, summoned up more puns, in a sort of desperation, in one week than in any year of my life.' His nurse said he died with a pun on his lips, but she didn't understand the reference, so it has been lost.

Perhaps in reaction to the seriousness which had accompanied their suppression, punsters in the nineteenth century embraced the exceptionally silly, the absurd. Edward Lear's nonsense poetry barrels along under the weight of tons of puns, and Victorian burlesque writers revelled in the most childish, obvious paranomasia. *Punch* featured many contributors who punned incessantly to the delight of its readers. Punning was seen as wit for the masses. Truly vile puns were inscribed on everything from plates and tobacco jars to postcards and pillows, the way Pocahontas T-shirts and other McRubbish are merchandised today.

And then came Lewis Carroll, who returned the pun to its former glory, even while his work epitomised the absurd. As we mentioned earlier, his stories and poems, including *Jabberwocky*, *Alice in Wonderland*, and *Alice Through the Looking Glass* were distinguished by every manner of pun from antanaclasis to portmanteau. In *Alice Through the Looking Glass*, Humpty Dumpty is a wild punster, while Alice is conservative, nervous, and pedantic about words. After displaying his punnical prowess he tells Alice that, 'When I make a word do a lot of work like that, I always pay extra.' Here he exhibits the kind of esteem most punsters have for words, in spite of their apparent disrespect. But not the snark. As the King says, a snark 'always looks grave at a pun'. Even though Carroll is obviously hot for the pun, he knows one can go too far with it. With the Gnat, he personifies the serial punster—gnat one to let a pun go by—who mercilessly tortures Alice with puns and then actually dies from a pun himself. In *Alice in Wonderland*, Carroll recreates a dreamscape which is literally built with puns. The school of fish, as mentioned, is a visual pun which is then filled with verbal puns, including 'reeling' and 'writhing' for 'reading' and 'writing'. Supposedly he wasn't a drug-user, but come on.

Across the Atlantic, the Yanks were pumping out punsters in the grand tradition. The first noteworthy American literary punster was Edgar Allan Poe, who probably started punning when he worked in a newspaper office. His poetry is also peppered with some lovely plays on words, such as:

> Even the bright extremes of joy
> Bring on conclusions of disgust,
> Like the sweet blossoms of the May,
> Whose fragrance ends in must.

We're sure you got the double meaning of 'May' and 'must' ('May' meaning both the month and 'might', and 'must' meaning both mould and 'has to') but we thought we'd spell it out just this once, in case English is your second language or you're from another solar system. Anyway, Poe was everything you'd expect of a shameless punster—he was an alcoholic who did lots of drugs and even married his thirteen-year-old cousin, just like Jerry Lee Lewis. And in his spare time, he formulated the short story as we know it today and invented detective fiction. Goodness gracious, great balls of ire.

The next major American pun-freak was Henry David Thoreau, the eccentric's eccentric. Not only was he a friend and defender of chipmunks and radical activists alike, he wrote *Civil Disobedience* which is certainly in the spirit of the pun even if it contains only a few. But in *Walden*, his beautifully composed literary masterpiece, Thoreau created one of the great pun-propelled works, probably exceeded only by Joyce's *Finnegans Wake*. *Walden* is a parable and everything in it has a double meaning expressed in puns. Get into it. Tolstoy and Ghandi did, and never looked back.

And then everybody got in on the act. Americans, the English—even Oscar Wilde, that paragon of wit, punned in his title, *The Importance of Being Earnest*. All the right outcasts were doing it. But especially the Irish. The twentieth century saw the arrival of the great Irish punsters, led by that most 'out there' paranomaniac, James Joyce who, like Shakespeare, will be exposed in all his primal punning glory in his own chapter.

Like Joyce, the rest of the Irish punsters were iconoclastic in the extreme, re-inventing literary forms and philosophies in between pints. Along with many others, Brendan Behan followed ably, though rarely in a straight line, in Joyce's footsteps. Beckett, the greatest existential punster, went so far as to replace God with the pun in describing life and the universe: 'What but an imperfect sense of humour could have made such a mess of chaos. In the beginning was the pun.' And this from the man who said he had no bone to pick with graveyards.

Punning was no longer the exclusive domain of the literary. Between Freud, Jung, and the rest of those guys, culture would never be the same. Psychology changed the way we saw ourselves, and the Surrealist movement in art used the visual pun to depict the unconscious. They used images the way words are used in the verbal pun, making bizarre associations and juxtapositions to reveal meaning, often humorously. And they occasionally resorted to the verbal pun. Marcel Duchamps' pseudonym was Rrose Sélavy which, if you say it right, sounds like '*Eros, c'est la vie*'.

In the meantime, eminent literary types held up their end. The poet, Robert Frost, considered himself a punster of the people—unusual to get a punster from California—and enjoyed using the pun to poke fun at literary sacred cows. In the tradition of his fellow American, nature lover and giant killer, Thoreau, Frost said, 'T.S. Eliot and I have our similarities and our differences. We are both poets and we both like to play. That's the similarity. The difference is this: I like to play euchre; he liked to play eucharist.' Touché Frosty.

Henry Miller deserves more than a footnote in a history of punning for the title of Volume One of his collection of erotic short stories, *Opus Pistorum*. The volume is called '*Sous les Toits de Paris*'. This translates literally as 'Under the Roofs of Paris', but of course 'Toits' sounds like 'twats', which is at least as much to the point. Interestingly, Shakespeare used the word 'roof' to refer to female genitals, and as no dictionary can tell us where the word 'twat' came from, we suspect it could have been a French crossover somewhere in the seventeenth century. *Peut-être*.

The second half of this century has been highlighted by some fantastic (in the orignal sense of the word) punster/novelists such as Anthony Burgess, Thomas Pynchon and Vladimir Nabokov. They each used characters who were in one way or another, different, if not downright perverted, to perpetrate their puns. This allowed them to get away with wordplay murder and depravity, a feat which can also be achieved by suggesting the dream state, the way Lewis Carroll or James Joyce did. As Burgess wrote, 'A deranged narrator, like those in Nabokov's *Lolita* and *Pale Fire*, can be entrusted with coinages like these. If the narrator is not deranged he had better be dreaming.' And if you want deranged in both pun and practice, read the narration by Burgess's 'hero' of his modern classic, *A Clockwork Orange*. Real horror show.

These days, the literary pun is pretty rare, which is probably more an effect of reading rather than writing habits. Whether we took a speed-reading course or not, most of us try to do it. We live in a supersonic, microwaved, amphetamine-driven world. Everything quickly digested and disposed of. That's what our lives have become, and it's a tragedy. We demand literature that spells out its meaning, unfettered by ambiguity or linguistic complexity. It's a cut-to-the-chase mentality. Why should we make the time to read the way we have to, to absorb sophisticated literary puns? In Shakespeare and Joyce and Nabokov, we have to read carefully, and *re-read*, if we're going to get even half of what they were on about. And the point is that it's worth it. There is so much wit and truth in what they have to say and the way they have to say it. It can be such a pleasure to savour each phrase and luxuriate in its meaning, once we understand what kind of trickery is at work. No doubt the pun will rise again. Perhaps we should move for its prohibition so that in their perverse way, punsters will be stimulated by the spirit of revolt. For the rest of us true believers, it's our party and we'll pun if we want to.

FISHING

If you bring your rod and reel to an empty stream,
it's fishin' impossible.

FOOD

The breakfast chef: the practical yolker.

Too much vegetarian food can make you pea-sick.

It tastes great on a hot day in January: a midsummer's ice cream.

Gay Asian Restaurant is called Sum Yung Guy.

The vegetarian cook to her boss: peas to meet you.

The baker used body parts and came up with the organ donut.

The baker told the apprentice who burned the bread,
'Better loaf well enough alone.'

Tale of two bakers who became mutually enamoured: Loaf Story.

The chef looked into the dark, damp cupboard and said,
'Not mushroom in here.'

Schizophrenic comestible: I ham what I yam.

The late breakfast chef pleaded, 'I bacon your pardon.'

Baker's song to lover: You Light Up My Loaf.

If you don't know what to put in the jam, then comquat may.

When the rabbi complained about his seafood
he explained: mussel tough.

The cooks working in a haunted bakery experienced fear and loafing.

Bad cooking: the pot thickens.

Baking can get tedious; a baker can be bored and bread.

Making good coffee every morning can be a grind.

The chef refused to cook just vegetarian; he'd bean there, done that.

When the Asian cook went beserk and shot seven customers for complaining about his soup, they called it a won ton act.

Words before vegetarian meal: lettuce pray.

FRIENDS

It's good to have a friend who likes to gossip;
they're valued for their keen sense of rumour.

But not necessarily friends who gossip about you;
with friends like them, who needs enemas?

When you're still pissed off with a friend you've fought with,
you're said to be side-by-snide.

The rich guy had a poor guy for a friend;
he treated him quite famillionairely.

If a friend tells you he's sorry he slept with your partner,
take it at farce value.

When you prefer your flatmate's date to your own,
you say, your guest is as good as mine.

GREENIES

Their message: Leaf well enough alone.

Conservationists want to protect the wetlands,
but others think it's marsh ado about nothing.

GYMNASTICS

Occasionally gymnasts fall on deft rears.

HEALTH

Someone who has laryngitis is a hoarse whisperer.

Hypochondriacs are fans of human bandage.

The woman suffered from very close veins.

One surgeon bragged to another: spleen there, done that.

Accident victim to doctor at derailment:
the pain in brain falls mainly under train.

Doctor to worried mother after treating her son: heal be all right.

When you've gotten over your bladder infection
you are said to pee no evil.

Gout victim: the node warrior.

Before they screened blood: the years of giving dangerously.

When the guy came out of tuberculosis therapy,
his friend said, 'Lung time no see.'

Mad cow: the steer of living dangerously.

KARMA

Time wounds all heels.

Driveway tragedy: my karma ran over my dogma.

LOGGERS

Their weekly info sheet is called The Chipping News.

To them, love is a many splintered thing.

MARINE LIFE

When your sea creature wants something in return for
his companionship he expects it to be squid pro quo.

Pushing an exhausted, beached dolphin back out in a
rough sea would be defeating the porpoise.

SHAKESPEARE

The Good, the Bard and the Ugly

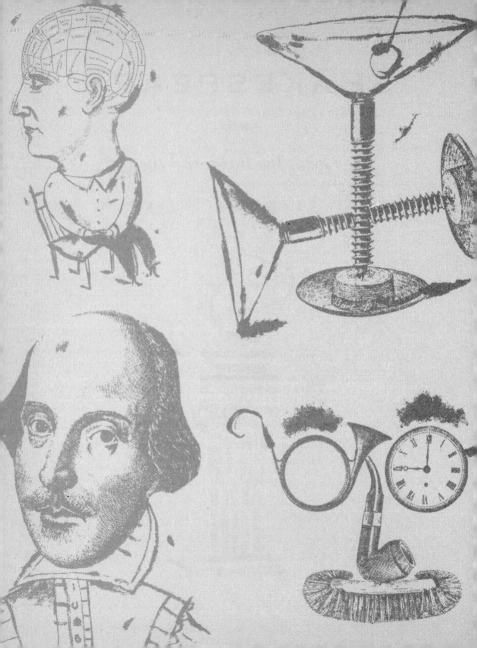

The most unstoppable literary punster of them all was William Shakespeare, whose very name comprises several potential puns which you'll be able to spot later, if you can't already. Between his name, his vocation and his era, the Bard was destined for punning glory. The pun was a pervasive (perversive?) element in Elizabethan society and literature. Members of court would amuse themselves for hours with formal contests of wit, especially punning. (They didn't have TV back then.) Wordplay overtook swordplay. As Shakespearean pun-chronicler, F.A. Bather said, 'In Shakespeare's day, the fine gentleman that could not turn his words inside out like a cheveril glove was esteemed but a poor fellow.' Punning was definitely 'in'.

Theorists suggest that the reason for the punning-vogue was the evolutionary stage of English itself. Having recently moved on to the next phase after Middle English, Elizabethan English was in the process of borrowing bits of Latin, French, and Greek among other tongues, courtesy of the Renaissance. Words carried new connotations, and English became a rich soil for the growth of puns. There was a ubiquitous sense of humus. It has been noted that bilingual societies or ones in which the language is in a state of flux become ripe for the punning, so Elizabethan English had all the right ingredients for a punfest. Bather agrees with our old nemesis, Addison, that at this point in the development of a language, writers are like children, happily playing with and deconstructing their new toy. Pigs in shit. As Bather describes young Will's punning propensity: 'In the exuberance of youth, his brain thick with teeming fancies, his mind impressed by the euphuistic style of the day, Shakespeare simply revelled in his mastery of language and was no doubt eager to show that, whatever others could do, he at any rate could go one better.' So, as always, there was a lot of literary dick-swinging, and Shakespeare wanted to prove that he had the biggest talent. Today he could have just bought a red Porsche and a mansion on the harbour, but instead he wrote the most beautiful, revered, performed, filmed and disgusting plays in the history of the language. And he punned profusely in every one of them.

Obviously Shakespeare had other reasons for punning. He recognised that the point of the pun is to compound the mean-

ing of words and phrases. It was economical for him and satisfying for the audience as it broadened the theatrical experience.
So punning wasn't just a wank. By playing with words, he was
communicating; the audience could solve his puzzles and get his
point. For today's audience or reader, getting into the puns is a
bit like opening Pandora's box. The quibbles fly at you from
every direction and challenge you to understand their many levels of meaning. But once you do, you will never again be content
with the face value of a line like the Nurse's to Romeo in *Romeo
and Juliet*: 'For Juliet's sake, for her sake, rise and stand.' She
didn't just mean, come and get her. The word 'sake' was a pun on
'sack', in this case Juliet's vaginal sack, and 'rise and stand'
referred to Romeo's erection. Trust us.

If you want to get most of Shakespeare's puns, it helps to use
a guidebook and there are a lot of them out there. But we'll give
you just a taste. Because we don't want to scare you off, we'll be
using some of the most obvious puns as examples—ones which
use words that actually sound like other words they mean to signify. But some of them are tricky because the puns use words with
outmoded meanings, for example in *King John* when the
Dauphin is being betrothed:

> King Philip: It likes us well; young princes, close your hands.
> Austria: And your lips too; for I am well assured that I did
>   so when I was first assured.

Back then, 'assured' meant engaged to be married, which you

might not have known. Another trick to watch out for is when Shakespeare puns on Latin, Greek and French words. In *The Comedy of Errors,* such a pun occurs:

> Antipholus of Ephesus: She shut the doors upon me,
> While she with harlots feasted.
> The Duke: A grievous fault!

In French, *grivoise* means licentious which referred back to 'harlots'. Bet you didn't catch that one. Maybe you didn't want to.

Bather actually counted the puns in Shakespeare's plays (we think Steve Martin used him as a model for *The Lonely Guy*), and came up with the grand total of one thousand and sixty two, although many more have since been identified. So, if you want to get all of them, remember those reference books. Actually, if you want to get all of them, you're weird.

The first thing to remember is that Shakespeare chose every word for a reason. As his Richard III said, 'I moralise two meanings in one word.' He often used puns to express the themes of a play, and whether the audience was conscious of it or not, the puns functioned in the realm of subtext. Sometimes, the punning is not perpetrated on the audience as much as it is on other characters in the plays. In *Twelfth Night,* the Clown repeatedly calls Olivia 'madonna': 'good Madonna, give me leave to prove you a fool'. She is nearly driven mad, if not proved a fool, as what he is really calling her is 'mad donna' or crazy lady. Hamlet does more than dabble in the quibble, and often hides his intent in his puns which the other characters, who would be very pissed off at his meaning, don't get. But the audience or reader gets it, so we are drawn into Hamlet's mind and apprised of his agenda. In *Romeo and Juliet*, Mercutio is another of the playwright's paranomaniacs who even puns as he is dying: 'Ask for me to-morrow and you shall find me a grave man.' Indeed, Shakespeare had no problem punning when death was at hand. Lady Macbeth says of murdered Duncan: 'If he do bleed, I'll gild the faces of the grooms withal; for it must seem their guilt.' A visual *and* verbal pun. Often, he sets up punning duels between lovers who are battling as they fall in love. *Love's Labour's Lost, Much Ado About Nothing,* and *The Taming of the Shrew* all blister with punning exchanges. The essential paradox of the pun perfectly reflects the lovers' conflicting emotions. One puns, and the other puns back. It's a way to test, and also to pleasure. Punplay as foreplay.

BUTT IS IT ART?

Anyone who still harbours the illusion that Shakespeare's plays are not among the raciest works in English literature need look no further than his puns to have their quaint misconceptions shattered. The guy made puns about incest, masturbation, sexual prowess, gays, lesbians, impotence, castration, hermaphrodites, farting, shitting, dildos, donkey-fuckers, catamites, mountains of 'straight' sex, and every body part ever employed in various sexual acts. If most people knew what Shakespeare was on about in his puns, his plays would be banned from every school library in the country. And of course this is one of the reasons to pun. But not only was it convenient to shield his meaning from the direct gaze of the censor, Shakespeare knew that sexual references can be more titillating when they are slightly less accessible. Hidden meaning can have a more profound effect than the obvious. That's why porn gets boring.

Some Shakespearean commentators, including Bather and that prolific doyen of wordplay, Eric Partridge, have challenged the view that a huge percentage of the bard's references were sexual. But they were far more uptight than Elizabethan audiences, who were not only used to incessant punning, but tolerated and *expected* a salacious slant on things. In London at the time, the theatre district was also home to its many and various brothels, which carried on their business in the open. Indeed, the owners of the Globe also owned several neighbourhood brothels. So, before seeing Shakespeare's latest offering, audiences would saunter past (sometimes *through*) everything from 'molly-houses'—male brothels—to bondage and discipline parlours for a little whoreplay.

No doubt these audiences understood and delighted in what to us might be some fairly confronting double-meanings in Shakespeare's language. So, a lot of the pretty poetry and characters often have a dark underbelly, which we'll give you a glimpse of now.

From *Love's Labour's Lost*, Boyet to the French ladies:

> Arm, wenches, arm! encounters mounted are
> Against your peace.

He wasn't just talking about the outbreak of war, but of rape. The word 'arm' commonly signified penis, and any word with the 'count' syllable in it frequently meant 'cunt'. 'Peace' was a pun on 'piece' which referred to genitalia. So, it wasn't just encounters he anticipated being mounted.

Here's a nice one from *Macbeth*. See if you can spot the puns:

> Lady Macbeth: Nought's had, all's spent,
>   Where our desire is got without content.

This one is a little tricky because it has to conjure up a mental image for the pun to work. 'Nought' means 'O' which Shakespeare intended to mean the vaginal orifice. 'All' punned on 'awl'—a pointed tool for pricking—which meant … you got it … penis.

'Spent' meant came. So, he was drawing a parallel between the sex act and the act of murder, in terms of lack of satisfaction. Very Woody Allen. The great themes don't change, do they?

Try this one from *Antony and Cleopatra*:

Cleopatra: ... Antony
 Will be himself.
Antony: But stirr'd by Cleopatra.

This is another one of those puns based on a French word. '*Bouger*' means to 'stir', and although it doesn't sound much like it, it *looks* like bugger. So 'stir' referred to sodomy, reinforced by the preceding 'but' which very often meant 'butt'. Speaking of buggery, Mercutio puns similarly in *Romeo and Juliet* when he says that he 'will not budge for no man's pleasure'. He'll not move *and* he'll not engage in sodomy, no matter who's asking.

From *The Taming of the Shrew,* you can surely get the one when Katherina tells the wives that a woman owes it to her husband to be 'obedient to his honest will' and 'kneel for peace'. That's right. She was supposed to kneel for *his* piece. She said a mouthful. So it's not so hard to understand once you get the hang of it. So to speak. And you can see that so much more meaning is folded into one phrase when a pun's at work.

This one might take a bit more of an effort. When King Lear talks of 'discarded fathers', he is actually describing them not only as abandoned but powerless. You see, 'card' was a pun on 'cod' or scrotum, so to 'discard' was to castrate. Discarded fathers were impotent as well as cast aside. Takes balls to write that.

When Othello says to Desdemona, 'If I court moe women, you'll couch with moe men,' he wasn't suggesting a double standard. 'Court' meant more than court, it was actually a pun on 'coit' or have sex. Either way, it all got them both in deep trouble. Sex usually does. When Sampson tells Gregory in *Romeo and Juliet*, 'I strike quickly, being moved', 'quickly' is a quick lay, as being moved meant to be sexually aroused. Hmm. We wonder how often Will got laid.

If you have a few months to fill, you might like to go through Shakespeare's plays and find all of his puns on the penis. This one from *The Life and Death of King Richard II* is fairly unsubtle:

> Lord Marshall: My Lord Aumerle, is Harry Hereford arm'd?
> Aumerle: Yea, at all points; and longs to enter in.

You have 'arm' as penis, 'all points' as awl points or penis, and of course 'long' as in desires and 'long' in length. This latent sexual metaphor for military penetration runs throughout the historical plays, and is quite easy to spot once your mind starts working along these lines.

This one is also pretty obvious:

> Othello: Come, Desdemona; I have but an hour
> Of love, of worldly matters and direction,
> To spend with thee.

Say it out loud: '... of worldly matters *and erection* ...'

It also shouldn't take a degree in philology to work out this one from *Love's Labour's Lost*:

> Costard: She's too hard for you at pricks sir; challenge her to
> bowl.
>
> Boyet: I fear too much rubbing.

If you thought they were only discussing archery and lawn bowls, you haven't been getting much lately.

In the poem, *Venus and Adonis,* one of the most common double meanings appears when the love-sick Venus …

> … hears no tidings of her love:
> She hearkens for his hounds and for his horn:
> Anon she hears them chant it lustily.

In case any of you missed it, 'horn' is still used both ways today. The word 'taper' was used in many of the plays to signify the male member, and here are a couple of examples:

From *Titus Andronicus*:

> Demetrius: I'll broach the tadpole on my rapier's point …
>
> Aaron: Sooner this sword shall plough thy bowels up …
> Now by the burning tapers of the sky
> That shone so brightly when this boy was got …

And this from *Richard II*:

> John of Gaunt: My oil-dried lamp … Shall be extinct with age …
> My inch of taper will be burnt and done.

So, you have to get used to the idea that a thing is not just a thing. It might also be the thing that it sounds like in English or

French or Latin, or it might be the thing that it looks like. For instance, an erection was commonly signified by 12 o'clock. Or 12 o'cock. From *Romeo and Juliet*: 'The bawdy hand of the dial is now upon the prick of noon.' That wasn't too obscure, was it? Or this from *Measure for Measure*:

Escalus: I will go darkly to work with her.
Lucio: That's the way; for women are light at midnight.

From *All's Well That Ends Well*, here comes one of those French-derived puns:

Mariana: ... promises, enticements, oaths, tokens, and all
              these engines of lust ... many a maid hath been
              seduced by them.

'*Engeancer*' means to breed, so in this case, engines of lust are penises.

In this speech from *Othello*, a whole bag full of *double entendres* endow Roderigo's words with greater meaning:

Roderigo: My money is almost spent. I have been tonight
               exceedingly well cudgelled ... the issue will be,
               I shall have so much experience for my pains.

'Spent' commonly meant discharged semen, 'exceedingly' referred to his seed, 'cudgelled' was about the sex act, 'issue' is both subject and offspring, and his 'pains' were his penis. Had enough?

Well, enough with penises and on to vaginas. In Shakespeare's puns about female pudenda, the word that is not used but referred to is usually 'cunt'. A typical quibble comes from *Romeo and Juliet* when Lady Capulet encourages Juliet to consider marriage:

> Lady Capulet: … Ladies of esteem,
> Are made already mothers: by my count,
> I was your mother much upon these years
> That you are now a maid.

'By my count' means both 'by my reckoning' and 'by my cunt', and Shakespeare uses this same pun several more times in the play. We bet they didn't explain *that* when you read the play in high school.

As usual, Shakespeare had as much use for a visual pun as a verbal one, and we have the benefit of both in one speech from *Cymbeline*:

> Iachimo: Your daughter's chastity … this her bracelet—
> O cunning, how I got it!

The bracelet and the 'O' are both meant to signify the vulva, and if you can't figure out what 'cunning' means by now, you'd better close the book and turn on the telly.

The same use of 'O's appear, with an added pun on 'fuck' and an interesting use of the word 'root' from Mrs Quickly (ahem) in the following snippet from *Merry Wives of Windsor*:

> Sir Hugh Evans: … What is the focative case, William?
> William: O—*vocativo*, O.

Sir Hugh Evans: Remember, William, focative is *caret*.
Mrs. Quickly: And that's a good root.

In *First Part of Henry IV*, a lovely combination of puns is uttered by Cardinal Beaufort when a truce is finally proclaimed:

Cardinal Beaufort: To ease your country… and suffer you to
                    breathe in fruitful peace.

'Country' refers to 'cunt' (in the nicest possible way), 'breathe' is 'breed' and 'peace' is once again 'piece' as in genitalia. So, through the use of these puns, the speech is about sexual congress and breeding, as well as the end of the war, or the outbreak of peace. The pun compels us to compare the two. Comparison through mutual reflection is the implicit function of the pun.

In *Twelfth Night*, the ring that usually refers to the female anatomy refers to the anus:

Olivia: Run after that same peevish messenger,
         The county's man: he left this ring behind him.

The use of the word 'county' suggests the guy's sexual ambiguity, confirmed by the 'ring *behind*'. It all makes sense when you realise that the messenger was a eunuch.

Moving right along to the bum, Shakespeare quibbled in a variety of ways about the human posterior. One of his favourites was to use the word 'arras' for 'arse'. Remember how many times things happened behind an arras? Well, you can bet your butt that a pun was intended. Like this one from *Much Ado About Nothing*:

> Borachio: I whipt me behind the arras, and there heard it
> agreed upon that the prince should woo
> Hero for himself …

In modern parlance, Borachio is being shown as an 'arse-wipe' as the 'whipt' means both whipped and wiped, and the arras is clearly the 'arse', emphasised with a 'behind'.

See if you can detect this one from *A Midsummer's Night Dream*:

> Prologue: … to show our simple skill,
> That is the true beginning of our end.

If you're up on your French, you know that '*trou*' is hole, particularly, the anus. So it's just a little bit of toilet humour, which craps up a lot in comedies like this one.

Here's a sneaky one from *Richard II*:

> Bishop of Carlisle: Marry, God forbid! … who sits here that is
> not Richard's subject? … That in a Christian
> climate souls refined should sho so
> heinous, black, obscene a deed!

Okay, which word in the speech rhymes with 'anus'? Precisely—'heinous'. The suggested comparison here is pretty obvious, yes?

Mercutio comes up with a good one in *Romeo and Juliet* which should be apparent if you've ever been to a French movie and stayed till the finish:

Nurse: My Fan, Peter.

Mercutio: Good Peter, to hide her face; for her fan's the fairer
          face.

Replace 'fan' with '*fin*' and Mercutio's simple joke about
Nurse's rear 'end' becomes clear. Often, a pun is a perfect
homonym to the one with the implicit meaning, like this one
from *The Comedy of Errors*:

Dromio of Ephesus: A man may break a word with you, sir,
                    and words are but wind,
                    Ay, and break it in your face,
                    so he break it not behind.

In this case, you undoubtedly got the fact that 'but' also means
'butt'. Butt wind, and its consequent references would have got a
lot of laughs back at the Globe, although its power to either
shock *or* amuse is probably limited today. Or maybe not.

While we're in the neighbourhood, we might just take a quick
peek at a few puns on testicles. Ouch. Anyway, open up that bottle of champagne at the back of the fridge if you get this one,
from *King John*:

King Philip: Our cannons' malice vainly shall be spent
              Against the invulnerable clouds of heaven.

Exactly! 'Malice' is a pun on '*malus*', which is Latin for 'apple',
so malice was apples, or balls. The cannons represented their
you-know-whats, therefore the point Phil was trying to make was

that they would be wasting their ammo in both a military and a manly sense. What will he think up next?

In *Julius Caesar*, more boys' games offer the opportunity for a pun in Brutus's question to Cassius:

> Brutus: … must I stand and crouch
> Under your testy humour?

What he really resented was being the crotch (crouch) under Cassius's testicles (testy humour), or power. An even more blatant example appears in *King Lear* when the effeminate Oswald is referred to as a '*detested* groom'.

Puns on the word 'whore' abound, using similar sounding words such as 'hour', 'horrid' and 'horse' among many others. Spot these from *Hamlet*:

> Hamlet: … He would … cleave the general ear with horrid speech
> … I … must, like a whore, unpack my heart with words …

And …

> Hamlet: … look you, how cheerfully my mother looks,
> And my father died within these two hours.
> Ophelia: Nay, 'tis twice two months, my lord.

He knew it was more than a couple of hours ago. The two 'hours' Hamlet refers to are apparently two whores, in this case, his mother and Claudius.

An explicit whore-pun crops up in *As You Like It*, when the Fool makes this cheery speech:

> Fool: And so, from hour to hour, we ripe and ripe,
> And then, from hour to hour, we rot and rot;
> And thereby hangs a tale.

The 'hour's are whores, 'ripe' is perhaps rape, and most certainly the hanging tale is a sick dick. Yuck.

The whore/disease connection was fairly big at the time, and it is punned on again in *The Taming of the Shrew*:

> Grumio: ... marry him to ... an old trot with ne'er a tooth in
> her head, though she have as many diseases as two
> and fifty horses.

So now that you understand how these most simple of Shakespeare's puns work in context, we'll give you a few more, out of context, which you will encounter on your own next time you experience the Bard ...

Stink/distinct ... eleven/leaven/raise/erection ... lean/*leno* (Latin for pimp) ... ole/soul ... hole/whole/holy ... merely/merrily (which meant sexually promiscuous) ... cunt/quaint ... whore/word/worse/war ... very/vary (bisexual) ... witness/*testis* (Latin for witness)/testicle/taste/twin/plums ... year/*annus* (Latin for year)/anus ... bad/*baeddel* (Old English for hermaphrodite) ... innocence/in a sense/in no sense/incense/in sins ... woo'd/wood/would ... neither/nether ... groan/groin ... traitor/trader (in flesh) ... ascend/arse end ... hence/hens (female

sexual partners) ... oft/aft/arse ... rarely/rearly (of the arse) ...
and finally a few more words for penis: post, plume, pudding,
tongue, torch, sceptre, seal, shin, chin, spirit (because in Greek,
keres is spirit and *keras* is horn ... but you knew that), spur, spurn,
stiff, taper, pricket, dagger, sword, pains, pinch, prick, pens, and
sting. And if so inclined, you can look for the rest yourself.

People have argued for centuries about whether or not
Shakespeare punned too much or whether he should have
punned at all, and their opinions often shed more light on their
own personalities than they do on the work of the playwright. In
1930, the British literary critic and so-called expert in ambiguity,
William Empson, suggested that Shakespeare's use of puns
'shows a lack of decision and will-power, a feminine pleasure in
yielding to the mesmerism of language, in getting one's way, if at
all, by deceit and flattery, for a poet to be so fearfully susceptible
to puns. Many of us could wish the Bard had been more manly in
his literary habits.' What a crock.

Frankly, we can't see a lot of fear in Shakespeare's susceptibil-
ity to the quibble, but Empson's fear of feminine pleasure is a bit
of a worry. If he wanted 'manly' he should have stuck with
Hemingway or just gone to a bullfight. We concur with one of the
great chroniclers of Shakespeare's puns, Frankie Rubenstein,
that both Empson and Samuel Johnson were wrong. Not only
were 'reason, propriety and truth' not sacrificed through puntifi-
cation (well, okay, maybe propriety), but levels of meaning and
humour were created which were deeply satisfying to experience.
Understanding Shakespeare's puns can be a breakthrough for

the modern reader/audience. Once you start to pick up on the obvious ones, they will lead to the more obscure. As that old pun-counter, Bather, said, 'Many a passage that was before dark and perhaps meaningless will have ... meaning and beauty.'

Everybody admits that the more Shakespeare wrote the less he punned. Even Bather believes that the poet eventually tired of incessant wordplay. Perhaps when the Bard matured he realised the errors of his ways and turned up his nose at the lowly pun as an embarrassing expression of his reckless and indulgent youth. Personally, we are most grateful that he didn't come to his senses any earlier.

<u>MARRIAGE</u>

The long and wounding road.

When the guy's blonde wife faded to brunette,
he sued for bleach of promise.

Alimony is the high cost of leaving.

One of the challenges of a marriage is dealing with
the martyr-in-law.

And then there's always the further-in-law.

You bed your wife.

After twenty years of marriage the wife thinks that
a thing of beauty is a boy to behold.

Divorce: the fleeing is mutual.

Inevitable trouble during a marriage is called a mid-wife crisis.

If there's some gender confusion at the computer dating service,
the problem may be the male oughta bride.

When you marry, your party days are over.

Sorry to put a wed blanket on everything.

When she finds out her husband is having an affair and
she's on her way to kill them both, it's wife in the fast lane.

Some people can't even speak to their mother-in-craw.

On your honeymoon there's lots to do, so get up bride and early.

When you go rock-climbing on your honeymoon
you risk wife and limb.

When the woman wants her slacker husband to
return she says, 'Loafer come back!'

When a sick guy marries his carer she's called a wed nurse.

When the cad's away, the spouse will play.

If the morning after your marriage you realise you want a sex
change, you might say you got up on the wrong side of the wed.

MATHEMATICIANS

The maths teacher who won't give you a passing
grade is a quantum creep.

MENSTRUATION

When the bloat comes in.

Woman with a long cycle is the seven year bitch.

MORALITY

Sometimes you have to add here to your principles.

<u>MUSIC</u>

The all-girl religious band is called Nuns 'n' Roses.

When some of the woodwinds arrive late for the concert,
flutes rush in.

A trio of street musicians are the Three Buskerteers.

The teenage boy thought girls would like him if he played the drums;
he thought they were sex cymbals.

That angel had a harp of gold.

You can tune a piano, but you can't tuna fish.

When the fat woodwind player tried to bully the little tuba player,
the latter said, piccolo on somebody your own size.

The pub where the string section always gets wasted
is known as the violin crumble bar.

When the string section rose up and strangled the brass section for
being out of tune, they called it a wanton act of violins.

Classical musicians are into group sex; two's timpani, three's a loud.

The percussionist preferred to live in the country;
he liked the cymbal things in life.

When a movie scorer is told to make it funnier,
he has to farce the music.

THE JOYCE IS YOURS

divider

The Cunning Punning
of a Devilish Irishman

The guy whom T.S. Eliot called 'the greatest master of language in English since Milton' was also the maddest punster literature has ever known. James Joyce's love of puns arose from his love of words, and he never missed an opportunity to make the verbal visual and vice versa. Near his writing desk, he had a view of Cork framed in cork. As simple as that joke is, it's indicative of the level of Joyce's thinking. Literary pedants have tried to sell the world the idea that his work is lofty, impenetrable—that his books take master's degrees to comprehend. Well, this is horse shit. Joyce was a writer for the people. His technique is often daunting, but his themes are not.

He wrote about stuff that everybody can understand: being lonely, being horny, being in love, being afraid, being broke, and being drunk. But he wanted his readers to experience his themes in an unconventional way, so he used words unconventionally.

Psychology had changed the way people saw their internal processes, and with Joyce that translated into a re-invention of literature. He broke all the old rules; he made up words, combined words, used onomatopoeia, juggled syntax, and had so much fun with symbols and references that his language sometimes becomes opaque. But the meaning behind the language is never opaque. Joyce was a showman, a dazzler, a classic Trickster who purposely deformed language to please and to mystify. He also played with words to make us conscious of them. As Bertolt Brecht did in the theatrical realm, Joyce reminds us of the artifice—that we are reading a book. At the same time, he exploits the magic of the semiological process to penetrate our unconscious. So, while our intellect strives rationally to solve his puzzles, his crazy constructs often allow his meaning to slip into our mind unnoticed. And puns grease the way.

Some of you may think that this is the kind of crap you're willing to put up with in poetry, but not in novels. But for a minute, try not to compare Joyce's books to the latest *Lethal Weapon*. Stop thinking, 'cut to the chase', and relax. You won't get the kind of action you're used to, but you *will* get action. And for a change, it won't just be the contrived car crash or happy ending handed to you on a silver platter, it will be your *own* intellect jumping through hoops and climbing jungle-gyms of wordplay at dizzying heights. The movie will be playing in your head instead of on the screen, and you'll be amazed at what your brain can do when you're pursuing one of Joyce's puns through a labyrinth of meaning and reference. Now we're talking 'action'.

Some scholars are underwhelmed by Joyce's puns, and believe that he was just showing off. Sure, there was an element of exhibitionism in his punning—after all, he *was* a Catholic and an Irishman—but he never let that worry him. To one critic of his puns he said, 'Yes, some of them are trivial and some of them are quadrivial.' So there. After his early work, which included *Dubliners* and *Portrait of the Artist As A Young Man*, Joyce shamelessly embraced his love of language and performed never-before-attempted feats of linguistic audacity, without a net. He was the Evil Kneivel of the literary world. In *Ulysses*, he virtually turned language into one of the characters and, as Burgess said, in *Finnegans Wake* perhaps the only character. The point is that you shouldn't be intimidated by the guy's reputation. Ultimately his books were intended as entertainments, not insults or insoluble puzzles. So get into them. And to preserve your sanity, you'd better start with *Ulysses*.

ULYSSES: PUNS ON PARADE

The most accomplished popular punster of this century, S.J. Perelman, said, 'I've come to realise over the years that *Ulysses* is the greatest work of the comic imagination that exists for me.' We tend to agree, and suggest that it is also a work of unmatched wholeness, harmony and radiance. Like a pun, the book exists on several levels. Every chapter represents a human body part, has a particular symbol and colour, signifies an art or science and uses a different stylistic technique. And you thought *you* were busy. It's also a celebration of Shakespeare, and a retelling of Homer's *Odyssey*. And of course it also tells the story of what happens in the life of Leopold Bloom, an Irish Jewish ad-space salesman, on 16 June 1904. Basically, it's about how an ordinary guy like Bloom has the same needs, passions, victories and defeats as an epic hero like Ulysses. That's all.

A lot of the writing is stream-of-consciousness which is meant to reflect the way the characters think. None of the writing is what you're used to. What you have to realise is that, unlike most novels, the meaning can't be comprehended by analysing the narrative—the characters and their actions. Instead, as the brilliant Joyce interpreter Stuart Gilbert wrote, the meaning of *Ulysses* is 'implicit in the technique of the various episodes, in nuances of language, in the thousand and one correspondences and allusions with which the book is studded'. Among Joyce's many technical jewels, puns shine brightly.

One of the central themes of *Ulysses* is resurrection or rebirth, and Joyce deconstructs the word itself fairly early on. Mrs Bloom asks her husband what a word in the book she's reading means: 'met him pike hoses'. Bloom reads the word—metempsychosis—and explains that it's from the Greek meaning the transmigration of souls. The word, his wife's deconstruction, and the various associated meanings haunt Bloom throughout the day. Punningly. It paves the way for a meld pun like 'contransmagnificandjew-bangtantiality' which refers among other things to the relationship between God and Christ—non-begetting father and unbegotten son—and Bloom and Stephen (who later become Stoom and Blephen). Or maybe that was just a sticky key on his typewriter.

If you want to find the section with the greatest density of puns, check out the 'Aeolus' episode, a.k.a. chapter seven. Blistering with puns and other perversions of language, it takes place in a newspaper office where Bloom has gone to do some business. Lenehan, the sportswriter (of course), personifies the punster in all his parasitical glory. He poses Bloom this riddle: 'What opera resembles a railway line? Answer: *The Rose of Castille* ... rows of cast steel.' Later, instead of 'damn clever', Lenehan cracks a metathesis when he says, 'Clamn dever.' But he's all style and no substance. Visual puns are conjured when he offers 'Sceptre' as his 'tip' to win the 'Ascot Gold Cup' horse race. The phallic and feminine sexual imagery are pretty obvious. But

Lenehan's Sceptre later loses. Impotent in defeat. Or in the horse's case, in de feet.

Throughout *Ulysses*, Joyce makes puns on his usual French and Latin words, but he gets even more obscure when he talks of 'Sir Lout'. Not only is 'lout' appropriately descriptive, but '*laut*' is the Malay word for sea. So the maritime reference is there, as is 'Sir Sea', otherwise spelled but identically pronounced in 'Circe', an episode in the novel corresponding to Homer's *Odyssey*. We're impressed.

In *Ulysses*, Joyce exploits the ambiguities of words and has a great time doing it. Others were not as amused. We can't be sure whether it was the jerking-off scene or the irrepressible punning in the novel, but it could have been either one that compelled the husband of a disgusted typist of the manuscript to burn an entire chapter. And even though he was at the time reviled by the public and mostly trashed by critics, Joyce didn't let them spoil his party. He went on to write a never-ending novel in a language based almost entirely on puns. And they still didn't lock him up. There's hope for us yet.

MY LIFE AS A ...

Dutchman: My Life as a Clog

Child: My Life as a Sprog

Porker: My Life as a Hog

Factory worker: My Life as a Cog

Amazed person: My Life as Agog

Person with narcolepsy: My Life as a Log

Beaten egg: My Life as a Nog

Slammer companion: My Life as a Pog

OPTIMISM

It'll all come out in the wish.

The best things in life are for me.

ORAL SEX

On your honeymoon it's nice to swallow one's bride.

Kiss and swell.

Mouth-to-south resuscitation.

Pick-up line: pleased to eat you.

If you're getting better head than you've ever had before,
you're at an all time blow.

Hitting blow the belt.

A woman said of her recently departed, well-endowed boyfriend:
he'll be a hard act to swallow.

Aural sex is heard but not obscene.

If you have *really* weird fantasies, you might like to eat your maker.

ORNITHOLOGY

The Mexican desert eagle is also called the Tequila Mockingbird.

Babes who treat you with contempt: The Scornbirds.

PERVING

An eye for a thigh.

If she's not wearing underwear, but her legs are closed,
you can't see the forest for the knees.

PETS

Children love little pet colonies. They give lots of love ant kisses.

Children will also get hours of enjoyment, especially in summer,
from their swimming poodle.

PLASTIC SURGERY

The procedure for elimination of unwanted sub-chin crepe:
halt-her neck.

Mastectomy conversation: breast left unsaid.

FINNEGANS WAKE: WE DARE YOU

In *Ulysses,* Joyce believed he had realised the potential of waking, or conscious English, so in his next book, he decided to 'put the language to sleep'. He had enough of what he called 'wideawake language' and 'cutandry' grammar. He wanted his oneiric narrative to reflect a world which doesn't make sense to the reader on a conscious level. So he figured he'd tap into the collective unconscious. You might call him an oneiromantic. As Anthony Burgess explains: 'When life is freed from the restrictions of time and space as it is in dreams, the mind makes less effort to sort out contradictions, or gentler ambiguities, and a word may ring freely, sounding all its harmonics. This free ringing in a zone of psychological experience which has all the doors open, may well set jangling all the phonetic and etymological associations which the mind is capable of accommodating …' Go ahead and re-read that bit if it didn't all sink in. Anyway, in *Finnegans Wake,* Joyce did what any red-blooded serial punster would do if he could: he created a new language based on puns.

Forget everything you ever learned or thought you knew about syntax, semantics, narrative, and character development. Try to open your mind as far as it can be opened to new forms of whatever can appear on a printed page. Remember your first acid trip. Now you might be getting close to where you have to be to get into *Finnegans Wake*. Probably the best way to experience this book would be while you're asleep and dreaming, but this is a little tricky to manage. Some of the greatest literary minds have tried to wrap their heads around this book, and only partially succeeded, if at all. Burgess writes: 'At odd moments in the last thirty years I have had a febrile conviction that I understood Joyce's deep meaning—usually in illness or the middle of the night. In waking health I remain ignorant.' We know we said Joyce isn't impenetrable, but we were talking about themes rather than language. *Finnegans Wake* is a bitch of a book and makes *Ulysses* seem like *Bananas In Pyjamas*. Robert Seidman, one of the writers of *Notes for Joyce*, advises readers to proceed to the *Wake* with caution. He says, 'The puns drive me crazy ... Too many levels of referents. I feel like I'm in a house of linguistic mirrors with a multiplicity of languages.' According to Burgess, 'To attempt a close analysis ... is to invite madness.' We're *so* scared. Not! Let's proceed—what are you, a wuss?

There are a few points that might help you through Joyce's macaronic word-jungle. The problem isn't as much semantic as referential. Linguistic experts have been known to give up on its dense and lumpy paranomania because they use their own body of etymological knowledge rather than Joyce's own life. The key to getting the thousands of 'in' jokes is in discovering the writer's personal references and preferences—his loves and hates, the places he went, the things he learned and the people he knew. Often, the references are so arcane, they're impossible to uncover without a library full of reference works in half a dozen languages including histories, bibles, cookbooks, fairytales, diaries, letters and phone books. You don't so much read *Finnegans Wake* as decode it. And even if you can, you *still* won't get a lot. But sometimes, the references are easy.

An unusually obvious example is the great wobbly body of Shakespeare references. Joyce worshipped William Shakespeare as much as he worshipped anything or anybody. To Joyce, the Bard was God. In *Finnegans Wake*, he refers to him as 'Great Shapesphere', and this is typical of his puns. By simply changing two letters he has done little to the word itself, but he has radically enhanced its meaning. He has defined his deity while also enfolding the book's theme of circularity.

Because the references are so many and so integrated, on a certain level the *Wake* is *about* Shakespeare. Not only did Joyce see him as the Creator, but he saw himself as the Bard's greatest, if not his *only* rival. Look for other pun-names which have meaning in context, such as 'Shikespower', 'Chickspeer', and 'Scheekspair'. Surely you won't be able to go past the phrases 'two genitalmen of Veruno' or 'Miss Somer's nice dream' without appreciating the allusions. Illusions? There are so many that you can start to go stark barking mad. The danger is in finding a Shakespearean punning reference in every bloody word or phrase. In the wake of the *Wake*, this could bring on a psychotic episode. As the character Haines says in *Ulysses*, 'Shakespeare is the happy hunting ground of all minds that have lost their balance.'

People talk about the labyrinthine word-jungle that is *Finnegans Wake*, but in fact, that isn't quite accurate. It will amaze, but it is not a maze. In mazes, there are cul-de-sacs—dead-ends with no way out except back where you came from. Joyce's pun-puzzles have perhaps the opposite problem; they lead you further and deeper into jungles of meaning and reference where no man except James Joyce has gone before. The only way out is to keep going forward.

To give you the basics, *Finnegans Wake* is a dream dreamt by a publican named Humphrey Chimpden Earwicker (who later becomes Carroll's punning Humpty Dumpty, among dozens of others) about his family and customers who each play different parts representing historical and mythical characters. In one night, the major phases in Western history are re-enacted. So, like *Ulysses,* the story is about universal experience. The *Wake* is about every war, every family, and every love affair that ever was. Sounds easy so far, right? Well, stay close. Joyce used the Italian philosopher Vico's model of history as a turning wheel to structure his tale. So it's circular; it has no beginning and no end. The last word of the book is meant to lead into the first word of the book so you can read it continually without pausing for the rest of your life. So cancel your subscription to cable, now.

Ambiguities and dualities abound in *Finnegans Wake*. It's definitely a value-for-money novel. Everything—words, people, events, images—is a kind of pun. Characters like Esther appear as 'sosies', or doubles of each other. '*Sosie*' is French based on 'Sosia', a character in Plautus who loved playing with mistaken identities. Another character, Isobel, likes to talk to her own reflection which comes to life when things get 'sosial'. It is not

irrelevant that Joyce's daughter, Lucia, spent her life in a sana-
torium suffering from schizophrenia. There is almost always
more than just one extra personality per individual, and the different levels can accommodate places and things as well as
people. Anna Livia Plurabelle ('Livia' being 'Liffey', 'Plura'
being plurality and 'belle' being female beauty) represents all
rivers and all women in the world. And the transmutations are
often cyclical. Finn MacCool is Finnegan the winegod is
Earwicker is Joyce is Ireland is God is father is son is Finn, again.
Each character hides a multitude of Finns. As Burgess explains,
'The piling on of extra connotations is of the essence of the
palimpsestuous—or palincestuous—technique.'

So, when we look at the puns in *Finnegans Wake* we are looking
at the pun as a literary device greatly expanded from its original
base. The puns are often obscure, rococo, full of verbal echoes,
multi-referential and of course sick or brilliant, depending on
your point of view. Joyce uses English, Gaelic, German, French,
Malay, Latin, Greek, and Dano-Norwegian to create puns. And
although the puns may be difficult to grasp, the ideas behind
them are usually not.

Some puns plucked from the prose and poetry … posies and
proetry … of *Finnegans Wake* …

Check out the title. Finnegan is a meld pun of Finn again, and
both Finnegan and Finn appear as characters. 'Wake' means
wake up, wake of a boat on water, and wake of a dead man.
Remember this is a dream; anything goes.

'The abnihilisation of the etym' refers to the atom bomb (the annihilation of the atom) and the end of things, but also to the beginning of things, or the creation of new forms out of nothing, '*ab nihilo*'. The circle of life. And the 'etym' isn't just the atom, but comes from the Greek root of etymology, *etymon*, which means 'true' as in the true or original meaning. See, that wasn't too painful.

When Joyce describes the singing Shaun as 'mielodorous' he manages to say three things: that he is melodious, that he smells like honey, and that under the honey he stinks.

The words Joyce coins, 'venissoon' and 'vanessy' mean venison and very soon and Inverness, with Shakespearean and Biblical references there for the finding.

Joyce can make a simple meld pun as he does with 'clapplaud' or he can perpetrate his more typical 'trivial', or three-pointed pun, as he does with with 'litterature'. There is the apparent meaning, creative writing, then the two meanings suggested by the deformed spelling, 'litter': biological offspring, and waste. The important thing, of course, is not merely that he established aural connections, but conceptual ones.

He uses 'erection' to mean both building and hard-on, and refers to a character who is 'acheseyeld'—apparently exiled, and with an ache. From the teensy bit of surface we've scratched in this book alone, you can understand Joyce's personal references in those puns.

When Earwicker is forced to mount his own defence he talks about the girls '… who would bare whiteness against me …' Not only is the ostensible meaning ('bear witness') implied in the pun, but the publican's parapraxis or Freudian slip is also revealing. He *wishes* they'd bare a little whiteness against him.

As the woman *and* Dublin's river, Anna Livia is said to 'cast her perils before our swains'. I don't think we need to spell that one out. If you don't get it, just go back to the chapter on pundamentals.

'The fall of a once wallstrait old parr is retaled early in bed and later on life down through all christian minstrelsy.' Re-read that phrase carefully if you need to. Remember that the novel is about Western history, and in this case, the fall of a god, so what event is the punning snippet referring to? Very good. 'Wallstrait' is Wall Street, and the fall is the Crash. The particular god is wealth, or Mammon, which rhymes with salmon, and a 'parr' is a young salmon. Maybe salmon ought to tell him to lighten up.

You have to start bringing out the reference books when you want to understand why a character is nicknamed 'Mildew Lisa'. You might not have known (off the top of your head) that '*Mild und leise* ...' are the first words that Isolde sings over Tristan's dead body in Wagner's work. So O'Mara, who is called 'Mildew Lisa', is associated with guilty love.

Another triple-whammy pun appears when a character returns from 'his penisolate war'. On a historical level it was the Peninsular War of Napoleon and Wellington. On a personal level, it was a war the character wages 'as late with his penis' (penis-o-late.) And then, on the writer's own level, it was a war waged with his 'pen in isolation' or exile (pen-isolate).

Some puns are musical, and one needs an advanced

knowledge of musical notation and mathematics to understand them. And bring your calculator.

Finnegans Wake is full of punning riddles, or conundrums, but we're not going to include any of them here because they're pretty involved. And you're looking tired. In fact, the question to one riddle runs uninterrupted for thirteen pages, so you can imagine what an explanation of the punchline would entail. (Our untimely demise.)

Joyce was especially fond of portmanteaux, and he really went to town with several which he invented for 'thunder', each of exactly one hundred letters. They are written with one letter following another, but Burgess suggests you break them up into vague lines of verse if you want to get the sense of them. Once more, we'll leave that to you for your next rainy weekend.

Maybe Joyce is full of shit. Did he really take his own prose seriously or was he just having a private joke at our expense? Maybe he wanted to see how far he could take even us lovers-of-the-pun before our backs were against the wall and we'd finally scream, 'Aw'right, aw'ready—we give up!' Maybe. But we don't think so. Some would say that this phrase from the *Wake* could be used to describe the basic conceit of the book: 'the hoax that jokes bilked'. You might think that Joyce was being too clever for his own good. But if that's the case, you still haven't surrendered to the dream-state in which you'll finally be able to hear the mesmerising musicality of the *Wake*'s poetry. So stop thinking. Stop trying to figure out what he means for a minute and whether or not anybody's watching, and just go with the flow. Rejoyce.

POLICE

When sending out the squad on a potential drug bust, they seek the help of their canine friends and announce: collie all cars.

When he pulls you over, a nice one will say, 'Police to meet you.'

In a broad-minded society, the policy is to police yourself.

POLITICS

A visit to Parliament is to go behind the schemes.

A Prime Minister is the Lyin' King.

PORNOGRAPHY

Vice and sleazy.

Don't secretly video-tape sex acts with your girlfriend; hell hath no fury like a woman porned.

The stripper was an artist: she did it with consummate tease.

Of Vice and Men.

X-rated movie queens: The Pornbirds.

X-rated film review: it was udderly titillating.

A pornographer is someone who gives a vice to the lovelorn.

The X-rated channel: Lay TV.

PRISON ESCAPE

When the woman passed a cake containing a nail file to
her convict boyfriend she explained, 'I baked your pardon.'

PSYCHIATRY

When you need to sedate a psychotic you hit the crackpot.

People who have had successful therapy once were worriers.

Cleopatra was the Queen of Denial.

Bio of a woman who lived with a psychopath: The Ding-a-ling and I.

PUNS

The life some of us lead: the loneliness of the long-distance punner.

If you haven't got a single one yet, then it's back to square pun.

The most satisfying things in life: puns and lovers.

When musicians do it, it's called band on the pun.

Before you go to work in the morning,
have a look in this book to have pun for the road.

After you've made love it's nice to know that the pun also rises.

If you aren't making any progress with your date,
try to hit 'em with the old pun-two.

The lowest form of humus; earthy wit that everyone digs.

Explanation of some humour: how the best was pun.

PUNS, THE
PRESS AND
ADVERTISING

To Write Roughshod Over

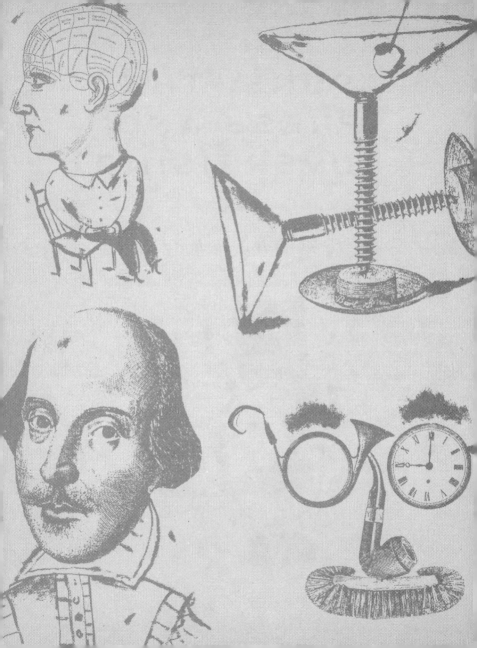

 Having established that there's a tendency for punsters to be sly, heavy-drinking, sex-mad, know-it-alls, is it surprising that journalism is full of them? Since the beginning of time, the press has been a haven—a smoke-filled barroom of witticism for those who pun. And the deadline seems to be part of the allure. We suspect that they *like* having to write while looking down the barrel of a looming deadline. The extra frisson that pressure brings is all part of the speed-versus-language battle being constantly waged in the mind of the journalist.

Members of the Fourth Estate are the smiling assassins of the

English language. They'll get nice and familiar with it, and when it's not looking, out comes the hunting knife and there's a major bloodbath. And of course the language isn't the only victim; it's the names in the news that really suffer. Often, the pun is the journalist's weapon of choice—the linguistic brass-knuckles which inflict an emotional black eye, so when the bruising's gone the pain (the pun?) remains. The daily newspapers are especially good at this. Puns in big bold type festoon the pages like bunting at a mafia wedding. And gone are the days of fawning obsequiousness.

Prime example, the monarchy. The British rags have had a pun-fest with the Royals. When the Princess of Wales is rumoured to have had an affair with a football player, it's: WILL MEET AGAIN! Or when speculation mounts that Charles may never become king: HEIR TODAY, GONE TOMORROW! And when the Monarch's manservant is photographed wearing suspenders and stockings it's: HOW QUEEN WAS MY VALET! When they forgo the pun and go for a straight line to comment on that big-eared prince having it off with a plummy housefrau, it's simply: YOU ROTTEN BASTARD! Doesn't have the same zing to it without a pun. It was nice to see these guardians of royal protocol return to the pun when Paul Keating put his hand on the Queen's back: THE LIZARD OF OZ!

And don't they love the exclamation mark! You've got to admire them for using it to highlight something that's already glowing like Chernobyl reactor No. 4. Our man in Fleet Street is never one for understatement. We'll lay heavy money that in some dungeon at the 20th Century Fox offices, Rupert Murdoch has an altar devoted to the pun lit by candlesticks shaped like exclamation marks.

Sport is another area that has always offered the press some golden pun opportunities. After all, sport heightens one's emotions, and there's nothing a punster likes more than needling an excitable person into a frenzy. For example, when Australia invariably has a batting collapse during a cricket test in the West Indies, out comes the headline: COLLAPSO! Or when Greg Norman wins a golf tournament, it's: NORMAN'S CONQUEST (no exclamation mark because golf is for people who aren't allowed to get excited).

Of course with puns it's easy to pick on the defenceless, the athletic, and Royalty. It wasn't always that way. Until the early sixties, most British newspapers banned puns because they thought readers might not get them. (The newspapers or the puns, we're not sure.) Nowadays, puns are used so often that they're the norm rather than the exception. Are newspaper buyers getting smarter, more witty? We think not. We suspect that editors either got bored or finally recognised readers' need to have some humour injected into their mostly grim news.

But it isn't always smooth sailing for punning journos. A pun aimed quite harmlessly at a presumably inoffensive target can come back to haunt you. Robert Cockburn, a respected correspondent and habitual punster for the London *Times* wrote an article for a flying magazine regarding the potential merger of an Italian aeronautics company with British helicopter manufacturer, Westland. The heading, SPAGHETTI WESTLAND? had the required effect. Law suits were traded like Alan Bond's art collection, but Mr Cockburn was finally vindicated and had the final say on the matter. He stated in a subsequent article that the sordid affair was PASTA JOKE.

Often the main pun-perpetrator on a newspaper is of course the sub-editor. This person is sometimes depicted as a hunchbacked, crotchety, half-blind troll, and this is only rarely the case. But he does mine endless pages of text looking for the Hope diamond of journalism, the headline. He is fully aware that a snappy one can have an impact on sales, and he will often go for a pun to make it work. Here are some headlines that won Walkley Awards for Journalism...

Robert Walsh headed a story about a cheese company paying the local council a fee to lay pipe:

$50 FOR RIGHT OF WHEY

James Main captioned a photo of boxer, Max Cohen, being decked in a prize fight:

COHEN, GOING, GONE

Richard Palk placed a heading over a story on unsuccessful rain dancers:

THE RAIN WAS PLAINLY ON THE WANE

In 1980 John Durkin headed a story on Treasurer John Howard's stern speech to state premiers on the need for fiscal restraint as:

SERMON ON THE AMOUNT

Robin Howlett headed an article about the close proximity of
a brothel to a police station like this:

PROS AND CONSTABLES

The former sub-editor on *The Age*, John Kiely, is no great fan
of the pun: 'I'll allow the occasional one but it has to be exceptional. Puns quickly degenerate into puerility.' This demolition
job didn't stop him from winning awards for his puns, so we figure he's a good guy deep down.

We're not sure Mr Kiely would like working on the *Sydney
Morning Herald*, which is far and away the Australian Mecca of
journalistic puns. But we're sure he'd mecca the most of things.
Sometimes we wonder if the *SMH* has a pun quota for each edi-
tion, there are so many. Such as …

A plea by scientists to refrain from killing the harmless
Bogong moths during their migration through Sydney:

LET BOGONGS BE BOGONGS

A takeover bid by Korean car-maker Daewoo of prestige
British cars:

LOTUS HEARS SEOUL MUSIC

A change in the high school English curriculum:

STUDENTS' POETRY COURSE TAKES A TURN FOR THE VERSE

An article on Emma Thompson mixing the financial success
of acting with the serious concerns of screenwriting:

CENTS AND SENSIBILITY

A piece on the demise of couture designs:
IT SEEMS FASHION'S BEING HIT WHERE IT HAUTES

An article on the opening of the Olympic rowing course at Penrith Lakes:
ROWERS DECLARE NEW OLYMPIC SITE OARSOME

A Pacific island nation goes bankrupt:
THE CROOK ISLANDS

One story can suggest a neverending flood of puns. If there happens to be widespread death, destruction or panic involved, then the pun can help to deflect some of the trauma. The outbreak of Mad Cow disease in the United Kingdom is such a story ...

When it looked as though every cow in Britain might be slaughtered:
LOTS AT STEAK

A caption of a photo showing a man eating beef:
COW COULD YOU!

An article on the potential ruin faced by farmers:
BEEF INDUSTRY IN A STEW

Another warning:
THINK BEEFORE YOU EAT

A piece on the tremors that occur:
OX I DANCE WILL HAPPEN

It helps if you're laughing when you wonder whether you might have eaten something with British beef in it and end up an oxymoron yourself.

Our friends across the Tasman aren't too shabby at the punning headline either. A beauty is from a newspaper in the South Island of New Zealand which covered the running aground of a coal carrier, the *King George V*, which refused to budge from a sandbar until five heavyweight tug boats did the job. The headline?

KING GEORGE V PULLED OFF
FIVE TUGS DID IT

Either that was just dumb luck, or there's an extraordinary punster loose in the land of the Wrong White Crowd.

Newspapers are certainly not the only sources of punning journalism, and indeed fashion magazines are at least as enthusiastic with the pun. These headings speak for themselves ...

BRIGHT LIGHTS BIG PRETTY, WILD AT HAUTE, STASH AND CARRY, GET GLOWING, BREAST FRIENDS, SCENTS AND SENSIBILITY, PEEKING KNEES, THE NEW WAIF, HEAVEN SCENT, GETTING WAISTED, FROCK AROUND THE CLOCK, SEX KNITTENS, POUT AND ABOUT, SCARF YOUR LUCK

We don't have a huge problem with these types of headlines, it's just that they're a bit cheesy. It's only when we leave the world of fashion and beauty and descend into sex, relationships, and modern living that the paranomastic headlines get down …

When every boyfriend is a jerk: THE DUD, THE BAD AND THE UGLY
How to keep a friend: BUDDY BUILDERS
When your bikini line is more like a jungle: SEXUAL HAIRASSMENT
Infections: THE YEAST OF YOUR PROBLEMS
Cellulite and its control: THE BUTT STOPS HERE
The mother-in-law hates you: BRIDE AND PREJUDICE
A dud bonk: BED COMPANY
He may have given you something: TO ITCH HIS OWN
Why humour is sexy: THE LUST LAUGH

We love the press because every day they churn out hundreds of new puns for us to chuckle at. (We don't sigh—we've groan out of that.) Even when the puns are terribly lame, it's confirmation that wordplay is alive and well (okay, alive) and busily fermenting in the minds of those who reach large numbers of people. And journalists are living proof that you can regularly hammer your mind and body with every known intoxicant and still crack jokes. And if you've ever been in a scummy bar in New York with some ex-pat Aussie journo telling you a shaggy dog story that ends with the punchline, 'ARTIE CHOKES 3 FOR $2 AT WOOLWORTHS', you'll appreciate the service they perform for society. They are the smelly sheepdogs that tenderly guard their flock. To which we say, get the flock out of here.

ALL'S SWILL THAT ENDS SELL

Puns make sense in advertising for two reasons:
1. ad space costs money, so the more meaning for fewer words the better, and
2. puns can be the lowest common denominator via the cliché.

No industry relies on our shared clichés more than advertising, and puns are useful in making the old new again. Which, in advertising, is usually the point. How many times have you noticed the words 'new', 'fresh' and 'different' in an ad? We rest our case.

That tired old chestnut, 'fit for a queen' got a perfect re-fit courtesy of the pun recently when the bathroom cleanser, Domestos, used a Terence-Stamp-in-drag look-alike in a *Priscilla*-style setting to make its claims. Suddenly an old cliché was hip, funny, and informative. An ad-person's dream.

Advertising targets emotional triggers that comfort us about our acquisitions. The goal is to conjure up memories of home-cooked meals and Christmas trees surrounded with presents—every one a product on which you can depend. So the punned cliché is tailor made. Like the way it's used in the ad for haemorrhoid treatment: MUSIC TO YOUR REAR. There butt for the grace of God go we.

So ad people pun all the time, but strangely they deny it. Maybe not so strange. Essentially, most copywriters want to be known more for their mercurial brilliance, their eighteen-year-old lover and their vintage Mercedes rather than the humble pun. But when they're sweating on the right line and way past deadline, they lunge for the pun like a life-preserver in heavy seas. But most of the time, they look at the pun as if it were the clap ('Oh my God, I've got punnorrhoea!'). Deep down they know that it's perfect for getting the job done. People don't sit down and read ads, they glimpse them from speeding trains or glance at them briefly in between bits of 'real' text. So whatever words ads use had better be eye-catching. Puns are great because they can force the double-take.

And even if they don't publicly admit to the effectiveness of puns in their ads, agency people use them privately. When a creative type we know fell madly in lust with a mail room boy, the latter was dubbed 'Dispatchcock' by the rest of the agency. This sort of wordplay goes with the territory. It's inevitable. We'd like advertising punsters more if they just came out of the closet and admitted that advertising is a big canvas, and that many creative brush strokes make the big picture. (Do we get the account?)

When a pun *is* used in an ad, it's usually memorable, therefore effective. Like the ad for Peugeot's new small car hailed as: THE HATCHBACK OF NOTRE DAME. The phrase has that eye-catching, double-take-inducing factor. And more than one message is delivered to humorous effect. Also, it demonstrates the client's desire to avoid the hard sell (a rare occurrence) and to treat customers as if they're semi-intelligent (even more rare).

The same sort of dynamic is at work in an ad for holidays in

Coffs Harbour, just south of the Queensland border: COFFS, NOT COLDS. Simple. To the point. A pun.

Likewise this one for a depilatory cream which also employs a good old cliché: HAIR TODAY, GONE TOMORROW. Moses first made that pun but it keeps on popping up.

The warm and cosy feeling is conveyed in this successful line about the motherly deodorant: EVERY GIRL NEEDS HER MUM.

The simplicity and allure of the pun can be seen in this ad for a definitely not see-through beer: COOPERS. CLOUDY, BUT FINE. And another beer ad, this one from England, where the advertiser has obviously targeted the blokesy end of the market for their strong brew: NEWCASTLE BROWN ALE—EVEN IN A CAN IT'S GOT BOTTLE.

Who says puns can't be politically correct? These two ads feature the environmentally aware pun: DO SOMETHING CONCRETE. PLANT A TREE. And: THE EFFLUENT SOCIETY: HOW CAN WE HELP CLEAN IT UP? This one is probably less ecologically sound, but it get the point across: ARE WEEDS A PAIN IN YOUR GRASS?

And of course there is the pun for a product on the name of *another* product appealing to the same demographic, exhibiting advertising's admirable tendency to feed on itself. Underneath a picture of a monstrous teenage pimple: FACE INVADER.

Undoubtedly there have been many great ideas for ads that have fallen by the wayside *because* they were puns. When will they learn?

We think there should be an ad for gym gear featuring Mick Jagger with the copy: LYCRA ROLLING STONE.

And we all know Toilet Duck, that helpful bathroom cleanser.

But how many people know that wasn't its original name? They probably thought of calling it STOOL PIGEON or TURD OF PARADISE or BOGHORN LEGHORN or COCKAPOO or PEE EAGLE. It is unbelieveable that some conservative market researchers must have poopooed these ideas.

So, while the needs of advertisers can be perfectly met by clever puns, it doesn't happen often enough. But you can help. Get into advertising. Flood the airwaves with cool puns. Before long your eighteen-year-old lover will get out of the Merc and say, 'You write up my life.'

RELIGION

When the guy talked the future mother of Christ into sleeping with him and later claimed it was the Holy Ghost, he explained that it was custom, Mary. She thought it was virgin on the ridiculous, but she did it anyway, saying that she'd try anything, dunce.

The priest who liked to tie the nun up with her rosaries had a motto: in God we truss.

When Jesus was tied up on the cross, the Roman centurion thought he said, '*Hole* my hand.'

Jim Baker-style religion: Lord love a buck.

An atheist is someone with no invisible means of support.

Many Catholics have 'lapsed' because they feel the Church is mass ado about nothing.

Fear of religious residences: cloisterphobia.

Adam and Eve were thrown out for Eden an apple.

The Lutheran who had sex twice on Sunday was called the boned-again Christian.

SCIENCE FICTION

Captain Picard baldly goes where no man has gone before.

SEX (GENERAL)

Spanking to you masochists: music to your rears.

A person who has intercourse without a condom can be die-sexual.

At an orgy in the dark the guy called out, 'Whose wife is it, anyway?'

An affair: The Fling and I.

Abstinence makes the part grow harder.

When she lowers her breast on to your face
she's being cone descending.

Heavy petting is the moisture fun you can have with your clothes on.

Ex-lovers: paramours lost.

When it comes to extra-marital affairs,
where there's poke there's ire.

Some guys will sleep with anything;
there's no accounting for testes.

At an orgy, east is eat and west is wet.

If you want to get romantic with a girl, keep a stiff up her hip.

The available one is called the lay teacher.

If he likes to talk dirty during sex he's a kissin' cussin'.

Suggestion that your partner undress
at the same time: bare with me.

He robbed his favourite prostitute;
she was the greatest whore he ever rolled.

When your girlfriend asks you if you're interested
in a little romance, raise your gland.

A group of hookers is an anthology of pros.

When you have a fight with your partner over one of you screwing around, suggest you get together and sordid out.

Incest on the farm: pump kin.

If you reveal all after a golden shower you like to piss and tell.

When the masochist reminded the sadist not to lose the keys to the handcuffs, the latter said, 'Truss you to think of that.'

A 'leg man' says, 'Thigh, there's the rub.'

When the priest pulled out of the nun just before he came it was semen on the mount.

If you're going to sleep with a total moron, just do it dunce in a lifetime.

When the prostitute told her client he missed his booking she said, 'Eh, Jack, you late.'

Movie featuring the multiple orgasm: Comelot.

Small orgy: itty-bitty gang bang.

Begging for bondage: please re-leash me.

Sex: twat's love got to do with it?

If your girlfriend accuses you of thinking through your faithless dick, stand by your gland.

Erotic dreamer: I dream of weenie.

Many brothels offer round-the-cock service.

Out-of-control orgy: when they come down
on you like a ton of pricks.

One of the great natural wonders of the
world is a woman's gland canyon.

The masochist cowered when he saw the dominatrix's whip,
and she told him, 'That's the leash of your worries.'

If you'd pay anything to sleep with the star of *Legends of the Fall*,
you'd be throwing good money after Brad.

THE GREAT PUN
BREEDING
GROUND

New York in the Thirties

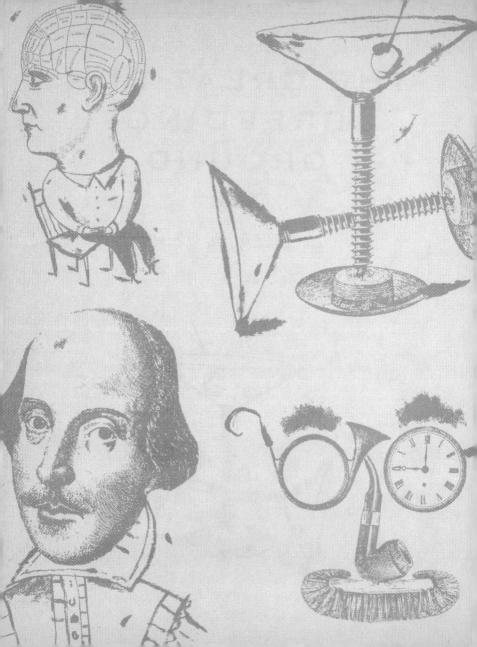

The blend of immigrant cultures and languages, the repeal of Prohibition and the Wall Street Crash turned New York into a hotbed of paranomasia in the 1930s. Or maybe it was just something in the water. Fuelled by legal booze, Jewish humour and the kind of ironic cynicism that follows a man-made disaster, writers and performers in the Big Bad Apple turned logically to the pun. A perfect expression for their audacious sarcasm, the pun experienced a heyday in the hands of a concentrated group of wits so intense they were scary. Until the outbreak of World War II, these punsters made the world safe for punning and some of their acts of linguistic heroism are described in the following pages. Our hats are off to them.

THE MARX BROTHERS

❧ or ❧

'Why a Duck?'

No book on puns would be complete without a section dedicated to the Marx Brothers. Combined with their mad physical antics and constant molesting of female co-stars, it's their machine-gun quips studded with puns for which they are remembered. And no wonder. Their background reads like a pun training manual.

Children of Jewish migrants to America early this century, they grew up playing with a new language in a community where comic relief was essential to get by. They had an archetypal stage mother named Minnie who made them each learn a musical instrument. This probably didn't hurt their sense of timing. And they had Mr Malaprop for a father. He once asked Harpo, 'Can I borrow your ducks tonight?' Harpo: 'My tux, you mean. What for?' Marx Snr: 'I've got tickets to a previous.' How could the boys not grow up as punsters in that environment?

It wasn't long before Minnie pushed her sons toward vaudeville. Julius, Leonard, Arthur, Milton and Herbert soon ditched those useless names and called themselves Groucho, Chico, Harpo, Gummo and Zeppo. And why not? On musical hall stages they developed their routines. Groucho was the personification of the serial punster: smart, fast, sexually aggressive, cruel, compulsive with his puns. Chico personified the malaprop in his role as an Italian immigrant with minimal command of the English language, and Harpo silently perfected the visual pun. Pun heaven. Gummo realised early on that his duties lay elsewhere and Zeppo just hung around trying to hide his massive schnozz.

It's impossible to say for certain who is responsible for each of the puns in the Marx Brothers' films. They always had a gaggle of scriptwriters, including the brilliant punsters S.J. Perelman, and George S. Kaufman whom we'll tackle later. Of course, after the fact, everyone would take credit for the best lines. (In the grand tradition of generous punsters everywhere.) But the brothers were known to be pun makers in their own right, and had been ad-libbing from their earliest days on the stage. They got so bored doing eight shows a week that they rarely performed their own material the same way twice, and often punned on puns, especially Groucho and Chico. Groucho dedicated his biography, *Groucho and Me*, 'To these six masters without whose wise and witty words my life would have been even duller: Robert Benchley, George S. Kaufman, Ring Lardner, S.J. Perelman, James Thurber, E.B. White.' (Each and every one a punster.)

The Marx Brothers' first movie was an adaption of their stage hit, *The Cocoanuts*, written by George S. Kaufman and Morrie Ryskind. Although it wasn't great, it was different, and had all the ingredients which they eventually perfected. One reviewer called it, '… the funniest movie ever made'. Obviously the time was right for guys screwing around with puns. The same writers were responsible for their next film, *Animal Crackers*, which continued to see the brothers treat scripts with absolutely no respect. They constantly improvised their lines, going off on bizarre tangents which sometimes worked and sometimes didn't. Kaufman, who hated this, once jumped up on stage during rehearsals and said, 'Excuse me for interrupting but I thought for a minute I actually heard a line I wrote.'

The Marx Brothers treated everyone with a lack of respect. Their director on *Animal Crackers*, Victor Heerman, knew they could disappear at any moment, so he had four cells constructed in which they were chained in between takes. At first the brothers thought this was funny, then they thought it stank. Like caged tigers they escaped to maul the movie-going public.

In their films, the Marx Brothers' puns crash over the other players like waves on a stormy coastline. Essentially, *they* got to be funny, and everyone else got to play the straight man. There were four types of punning set-ups. The first featured Groucho as the central player who punned intentionally and independently of everyone around him. The second used the combination of Groucho's intentional puns and Chico's malapropisms to multiply the puns geometrically. The third highlighted Chico and his misinterpretations on his own. And the fourth starred Harpo and his wonderfully groan-worthy visual puns. Let's have a look at how each set-up played out.

On his own, Groucho made puns on anything and they usually had no connection to the narrative. In *The Cocoanuts*, apropos of just about nothing, he commented, 'Over here we're going to build an Eye and Ear hospital. That's going to be a sight for sore eyes.' In *Animal Crackers*, the exchange went like this:

Guest: Am I intruding?

Groucho: I should say you were intruding! Pardon me,
I should say you *are* intruding. I was using the sub-
junctive instead of the past tense. Yes, we're way
past tents. We're living in bungalows.

Classic punning. And this, just as lame, and yet irresistible:

Chandler: I'm going to South America. Do you have any suggestions?

Groucho: Where are you going?

Chandler: Urugay.

Groucho: You go Urugay and I'll go mine.

In *Horse Feathers,* there was a lot of Groucho's grandstanding.
Such as when he's giving a university lecture and he eyes a young
woman sitting uncomfortably in the front row: 'Where is my son?
Young lady, would you mind getting up so I can see the son rise?'
This sort of line is obviously scripted, but Groucho had a way of
delivering a pun perfectly, without ever flinching or waiting for
anyone to get it. The same sort of appealing arrogance is at work
in this exchange with one of Groucho's hardiest pun-victims,
Margaret Dumont, from *Duck Soup.* They hear music being
played:

Groucho: It sounds to me like mice.

Dumont: Mice? Mice don't play music.

Groucho: Oh yeah? What about the old maestro?

And this from the man who in 'real' life said that 'women should be obscene and not heard'.

In *At the Circus*, Chico played Groucho's straight man:

> Chico: The guy who hit Jeff on the head and knocked him out didn't like him.
>
> Groucho: Don't let's jump to concussions.

And again:

> Chico: Don't worry about him, he's muscle bound.
>
> Groucho: And I'm homeward bound.

But Groucho does it all on his own after doing a scene next to the monkey enclosure. When he turns to leave, he shakes the chimpanzee's hand and says, 'Goodbye, Mr Chimps.'

Any one of those could have been scripted, but the following exchange from *Animal Crackers* feels like vintage Groucho improvisation. Note the way he trips off on a tangent, and never really makes it back to earth:

> Groucho: I was sitting in front of the cabin, when I bagged six tigers.
>
> Dumont: Oh, Captain!
>
> Groucho: Six of the biggest tigers …
>
> Dumont: Captain, did you catch six tigers?
>
> Groucho: I … I bagged them. I bagged them to go away, but they hung around all afternoon. They were the most persistent tigers I've ever seen. The principal

> animals inhabiting the African jungle are Moose, Elks, and Knights of Pythias. Of course, you all know what a moose is, that's big game. The first day I shot two bucks. That was the biggest game we had. As I say, you all know what a moose is? A moose runs around the floor, eats cheese, and is chased by the cat. The Elks, on the other hand, live up in the hills and in the spring they come down for their annual convention. It is very interesting to watch them come to the water hole. And you should see them run when they find that it's only a water hole! They're looking for Elkohole.

The same sort of paranomania appears to be at work in another of Groucho's speeches from *Animal Crackers*:

> One morning I shot an elephant in my pyjamas. How he got in my pyjamas I don't know. Then we tried to remove the tusks, but they were embedded so firmly we couldn't budge them. Of course in Alabama it's easier because the Tuscaloosa. But that's entirely irrelephant to what I was talking about.

The second formula, which combined Groucho's paragrams with Chico's malapropisms or misunderstanding, is probably the funniest, because they never give you a chance to catch your breath in between the puns. A brief, simple example is from *The Cocoanuts*:

> Groucho: All along the river are the levies.

Chico: That's the Jewish neighborhood?
Groucho: We'll Passover that.

In this next exchange from *Horse Feathers*, the boys really hit their stride, and demonstrate brilliantly how puns are formed in a conversation:

Chico: Who are you?
Groucho: I'm fine thanks, who are you?
Chico: I'm fine too, but you can't come in unless you give the password.
Groucho: Well, what is the password?
Chico: Aw, no! You gotta tell me. Hey, I tell what I do. I give you three guesses ... It's the name of a fish.
Groucho: Is it Mary?
Chico: Ha ha! Atsa no fish!
Groucho: She isn't? Well, she drinks like one. Let me see ... is it sturgeon?
Chico: Ah, you crazy, sturgeon he's a doctor, cuts you open whenna you sick ... Now I give you one more chance.
Groucho: I got it! Haddock!
Chico: Atsa funny, I gotta haddock too.
Groucho: What do you take for a haddock?
Chico: Aspirin.

The same *modus operandi*, with an extra helping of *non sequiturs*, applies to another slice of dialogue, also from *Horse Feathers*:

Groucho: As you know, there is constant warfare between the red and white corpuscles. Now then, baboons, what is a corpuscle?

Chico: That's easy. First is a captain, then is a lieutenant, then is a corpuscle.

Groucho: That's fine. Why don't you bore a hole in yourself and let the sap run out? We now find ourselves among the Alps. The Alps are a very simple people living on a diet of rice and old shoes. Beyond the Alps lies more Alps and the Lord Alps those that Alp themselves ... Now, in studying your basic metabolism, we first listen to your hearts beat. And if your hearts beat anything but diamonds and clubs, it's because your partner is cheating. Or your wife.

I think we might detect a little ad-libbing on Groucho's part there. Imagine what it would be like to spend a few hours inside his mind. No wonder he drank.

The next punning set-up was simply Chico's malapropisms gone haywire, in which Groucho often had to play straight man for a change. Perhaps these jokes were so popular because much of the audience in those days were either recent immigrants themselves, or the children of immigrants. From *The Cocoanuts*:

Groucho: You know about auctions, don't you?

Chico: Sure, I come from Italy, on the Atlantic Auction.

From *Animal Crackers*:

Dumont: I play a little, just for small stakes.

Chico: Okay. We play for small stakes. And French fried potatoes?

In *Duck Soup*, Chico's malapropisms were on parade:

Chico: … What is it has a trunk, but no key, weighs 2,000 pounds and lives in a circus?

Prosecutor: That's irrelevant.

Chico: A relephant! Hey, that's the answer! There's a whole lotta elephants in the circus.

Minister: That sort of testimony we can eliminate.

Chico: Atsa fine. I'll take some.

Minister: You'll take what?

Chico: Eliminate. A nice, cool glass eliminate.

Feeling dizzy? Later on from the same movie …

Minister: Something must be done! War would mean a prohibitive increase in our taxes.

Chico: Hey, I got an uncle that lives in Taxes.

Minister: No, I'm talking about taxes—money, dollars.

Chico: Dollas! Atsa where my uncle lives. Dollas, Taxes!

Then there was the sweet, silent one who was responsible for the fourth kind of pun. And, from all reports, Harpo was the best-adjusted Marx brother. He managed (unlike the others) not to alienate all of his family and friends throughout his life with his obsessive-compulsive behaviour. And his puns were the most understated. In fact they weren't stated at all—Harpo was a master of the visual pun. From *Animal Crackers*:

> Chico: Got the flash[light]?
> Harpo pulls out a fish.
> Chico: No! No! Not a fish. The flash!
> Harpo pulls out a flute.
> Chico: No! The flash!
> Harpo pulls out playing cards.
> Chico: , No! Not a flush! The flash!

Also from *Animal Crackers*:

> Dumont: What games do you play?
> Chico: We play lotsa games. Blackjack. Soccer.
> Harpo goes to hit another woman over the head with a cosh,
> and Chico stops him in time.

In *Horse Feathers*, Chico and Harpo are trying to escape from a locked high-rise apartment. Harpo uses his noisy bike horn to communicate.

> Chico: We gotta get outta here. You gotta rope?
> Harpo: Honk!
> Chico: Atsa good. Tie on the bed, throw out the window.
> Harpo: Honk?
> Chico: Tie on the bed, throw out the window.
> Harpo puts his tie on the bed and throws ...
> (We don't need to explain.)

In *A Day at the Races*, a medical examination of a young lady is underway:

Groucho: Take her pulse!
Chico: Take her pulse!
Harpo takes her purse.

So, with their panoply of puns and other antics, the Marx Brothers' tours de farce left an indelible mark (more like a stain) which still affects the world of humour today. Many of the television, cartoons and movies we see have the brothers to thank for setting them on the right (write? trite? rote?) path. The Marx Brothers drive you mad, they don't make sense, they did some really dumb stuff, but you can't help loving them. We have nothing but fondle memories of them.

S.J. PERELMAN

⚜ or ⚜

'I Loved Him Like a Brothel.'

There are few popular humorists in the modern history of punning who so rightly deserve the accolades heaped upon Sidney Joseph Perelman. Woody Allen said, 'When you read Perelman and you're a young writer it's fatal because his style seeps into you. I thought they were the best and funniest things that I had ever read.'

Perelman once' said, 'My names and titles spring out of my lifetime devotion to puns.' And devotion it was. The man had absolutely no shame. He started his career as a cartoonist, but in his time at Brown University he shifted from the visual to the written. Afterwards, he combined the two when his cartoons were published nationally, like the one in which a Pasha inquires of his Grand Vizier, 'Who's been eating my Kurds and why?'

His first book, *Dawn Ginsbergh's Revenge*, published in 1929, was loaded with puns. Maybe Sid had the brain disorder that always gets attributed to funny guys by guys who aren't funny. Some were frighteningly elaborate: 'A knock at the door aroused Dawn from her lethargy. She hastily slipped it off and donned an abstraction. This was Dawn, flitting lightly from lethargy to abstraction and back to precipice again. Or from Beethoven to Bach and Bach to Bach again.' Ah, the impetuosity of youth!

Cheesy or not, it attracted the attention of Groucho Marx, who wrote the blurb for the book jacket: 'From the moment I picked up your book until I laid it down, I was convulsed with laughter. Someday I intend reading it.' He then commissioned Perelman and his friend, Will B. Johnstone, to conceive a scenario for a radio show the Marx Brothers were planning. At the time, Perelman wasn't sure he could handle the assignment, telling Groucho, 'I've never worked on a radio script.' Groucho replied, 'That's great! I can't imagine two people worse for the job!' They went on to write *Monkey Business* which they later adapted for the screen. So began one of the most fruitful and troubled punning collaborations of all time.

A native New Yorker, Perelman hated Hollywood. He called it 'a dreary industrial town controlled by hoodlums of enormous wealth, the ethical sense of a pack of jackals, and taste so degraded that it befouled everything it touched'. We're packing our bags. Much later, in the sixties, Sid wrote a teleplay based on one of his stories called *Malice In Wonderland*. It was about a psychiatrist who is mesmerised by Hollywood and slowly driven insane by its shallow nature. But when Perelman first arrived in Hollywood, he didn't know about all that yet.

After finishing a first draft of the screenplay for *Monkey Business* which was laced with puns, Perelman and Johnstone were summoned to a meeting. After being kept waiting for over an hour, and shit-scared at the thought of reading their script, Perelman (the designated narrator) found himself in a room with the Marx Brothers, twenty-four associates and family members, and five snarling dogs. Soon after Sid started, Harpo fell asleep, as did the dogs and several other people. But Sid didn't stop. The reading took an hour and a half. When he finally finished, you could have heard a pin drop. Chico turned to Groucho and said, 'What do you think?' Groucho replied, 'It stinks!' at which point everyone got up and left. The rewrite took five months and was a truly collaborative affair. (If Harpo's dogs had an agent they'd have gotten a screen credit.) And of course the film was a huge smash hit.

Perelman went on to work with the Marx Brothers again when he co-wrote *Horse Feathers*, one of their most pun-loaded screenplays, but that was enough. He said, 'I did two films with them, which is perhaps my greatest distinction in life, because anybody who ever worked on any picture for the Marx Brothers said he would rather be chained to a galley oar and lashed at ten minute intervals than ever work with those sons of bitches again.' Many critics thought Perelman was great at throwaway lines full of clever puns, but he had problems with the big picture. Groucho agreed: 'He could write a funny line, but never a script. When he was writing for us, he was working with four other men. He thought he was the greatest writer in the world and didn't want to be identified with comedians.'

For all their bitching and moaning at each other, Groucho and Sid Perelman had a friendship that lasted for decades. Sid would often stay with Groucho in Hollywood, and they'd often dine together in New York, enjoying unrelieved pun-fests at everyone else's expense. But they fought. They were both aggressive, moody, ego-driven and sexually voracious, although both could also be charming. Punsters or what? They both came from poor Jewish immigrants but affected the manner of the English upper class. They were right into it—funny looking guys in dapper suits and canes; they wanted to appear gentlemanly. (Gentilemanly?)

There has been much discussion about who masterminded the 'Groucho' screen persona. Many believed that it was an extension of Perelman, although George S. Kaufman had greater input. But it's true that Sid and Groucho were a mirror image of each other. The physical resemblance was so close that many people assumed that Groucho was just 'doing' Perelman. At the risk of reducing them to a glib rhetorical metaphor—yeah, let's go ahead—the two of them personified the duality of the pun.

They represented two levels; Groucho was the external expression, and Sid was the internal. And they were both intent on catching women in their wordy web, using the pun as an aphrodisiac. How successful they were is a matter of conjecture. Sid did a lot of talking about his conquests, which probably means he didn't get much. For his part, Perelman said, 'I am what Puritans scornfully call a womaniser. It's sort of a lay preacher.'

After he left the movie business, Perelman went on to gripe about his book publishers, which we see as a case of biting the hand that reads you. Puns featured heavily, as they did in his story, *The Importance of Healing Ernest*, which related to his nursing Hemingway back to health in some third world country. Just before publication Ernie decided to brush his teeth with a shotgun, sending Perelman into a panic about the timing of the impending story. This is strange, because he was always complaining that there was never enough marketing done on his books.

Perelman had bought a large country estate in Bucks County, Pennsylvania, and after years of renovations he wrote a book on the trials and tribulations of country living called *Acres and Pains*. It was well accepted, and included such groan-worthy passages as: 'I started wearing patched blue jeans and mopping my brow with a red banana. It was some time later I realised I should have been using a red bandana.'

Later on in life, Perelman became interested in the occult, particularly the Ouija board. He proved that puns can even come back from the dead when he tried to contact his late friend, Ring Lardner. Sid asked him what he thought of that year's World Series. The answer came back, 'What Serious? Are you series?'

The downside to the incredible talent of a guy like Perelman is that as he grew older he turned into a whinging, back-stabbing grump. But he was unique. In an article written for the *New Yorker* after Perelman's death, William Zinsser said he was '*sui generis* to a fault'. And he was funny, so we'll forgive him. He showed all the retarded character traits of a true punster; no one can argue that he shouldn't be *Magna Pun Laude* in his class.

GEORGE S. KAUFMAN, DOROTHY PARKER AND THE ALGONQUIN ROUND TABLE

Groucho Marx said that George S. Kaufman was the funniest man he'd ever known. He was also luminously intelligent, weird, a chronic punster and horny. (Producer Max Gordon called him 'a male nymphomaniac'.) He was also a commercial and critical success, writing a string of hit movies and plays, two of which won Pulitzer prizes. In addition, he was a reviewer of distinction and a savage wit. He once wrote of a young singer's performance, 'Guido Nazzo is nazzo guido', which became so popular that the man's career was almost destroyed. An example of the awesome power of the pun. Kaufman happened to be a nice guy (unusual for a punster) and gave him a part in one of his shows.

What an interesting chap. Neurotic about cleanliness, he hated physical contact (except, we suppose, when he was fucking like a rabbit on quaaludes). He was an insomniac, a hypochondriac, and otherwise pretty normal. He was a fanatical bridge player who couldn't bear partners with little skill. In one famous encounter, his partner knew he'd blown it and asked George how he would have played the hand. George replied, 'Under an assumed name.' He once said to a playwright, 'I understand your play is full of single entendre.' But the full might of his humour shone forth in his puns, typified in his review of a play by Clifford Odets: 'Odets, where is thy sting?'

During the twenties and thirties, Kaufman gravitated to a circle of writers who would meet for lunch (which often became dinner, then breakfast) at the shabby/genteel Algonquin Hotel in New York. There was a skewed socialist ethic at work at the Round Table. If you weren't funny and in possession of a fierce intellect, riches and status couldn't buy you a seat. (How unbelievably cool.) Of course if you were beautiful and bonking one of the chosen, you would be tolerated until the affair ended. Usually everyone would be talking at once, but occasionally they would take turns dazzling each other with wordplay, often punning from one to the other around the table. This 'A' list of intellectual and literary élite included George S. Kaufman, Edna Ferber, Ring Lardner, Alexander Woolcott, Robert Benchley, Harpo Marx and the deceptively diminutive Dorothy Parker.

Dorothy Parker was romantic, venomous, a brilliant punster and a heavy drinker. This toxic cocktail inspired the sort of comment she made regarding a young, not very bright actress at the Round Table who was having it off with one of her ex-lovers: 'You can lead a horticulture but you can't make her think.' She went through guys like tissues, but she was rarely seen, especially in later life, without one of a succession of adored dogs. Hence her statement: 'A girl's best friend is her mutter.' This is no surprise considering her dogged approach to life. When she heard that a female acquaintance of dubious moral fibre had broken her leg she quipped, 'She must have done it sliding down a barrister.'

She wrote a lot of poetry, but was never very proud of it, calling it trite and derivative. She described herself as '… always chasing Rimbauds'. Although it seems that she never consummated her relationship with Robert Benchley, whom she loved for much of her life, she influenced him in other ways. He neither drank nor punned when he first met her, but afterwards he wrote a book titled *Bed to Worse* and died of cirrhosis of the liver.

As magnificent as all this wordplay in one place sounds, there were drawbacks. Almost every member of the Round Table suffered from drug and alcohol addiction and/or acute emotional disorders. So it just goes to show you that there are occupational hazards for everything, even punning.

SEXUALLY TRANSMITTED DISEASE

A babe with the clap is a Poxy Lady.

We think pre-AIDS and yearn for the good old gays.

VD: Pubic Enemy Number One.

When the guy's doctor gave him a clean bill of health,
it was all in good testes.

Nothing to clap about.

Seasons greetings card to fellow sufferer: Herpe Xmas

SHIATSU

Getting knead in the back.

SHOWGIRLS

Beaver Las Vegas.

SIN

Don't be a goody-two-shoes; in this world, it's sinner-takes-all.

Everybody does the wrong thing, sinner or later.

A lie is aversion of the truth.

<u>SPAM</u>

I'm pink therefore I'm spam.

I stink therefore I'm spam.

I shrink therefore I'm spam.

I wank therefore I'm sperm.

<u>SPORTS</u>

You can't really swim off Bondi Beach anymore.
All you do is go through the motions.

Wrestling eunuchs: battle of the sexless.

Sailing is a social sport; you're surrounded by buoys and gulls.

A men's locker room is a penile colony.

What you yell after too many hours of cricket: man overbored!

Fair play is a fine idea, but when the match
is over there's won and only.

When you've fallen overboard you're swimmin'
on the verge of a nervous breakdown.

If you're skindiving and your air-tank runs out
you're in a life and breath situation.

Golf: the proof is in the putting.

If you get hit in the head with your board when
you're out in rough seas, it surfs you right.

STARS

Sign leading up to Mr Costner's bedroom: Stairway to Kevin.

If the star demands too many takes on a
movie set he's over re-acting.

The director told the big-budget star to act his age,
not his show-size.

The Duke's autobiography could have been called *Waxin' Wayne*.

Mr Kline's boyfriend likes to sing: Kevin, I'm in Kevin …

SYCOPHANCY

A sycophant is a person who stoops to concur.

TEA

If you like your Liverpudlian marsupial refreshment straight, then the
koala tea of Mersey is not strained.

MODERN
PUNSTERS

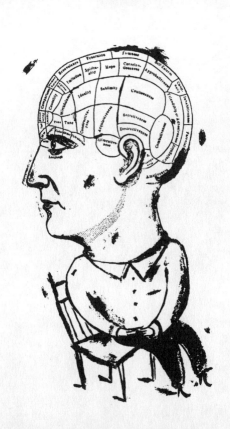

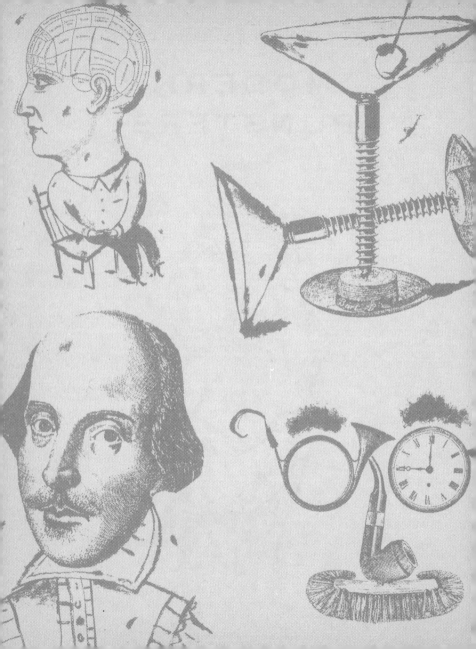

Who are the modern punsters? Well, as discussed earlier, a lot of them work for newspapers and ad agencies. Why write for obscure literary journals when you can make great money selling toilet paper? And the remaining full-time punsters are alive and well and working in movies and television. Through mass market entertainment, puns are now reaching more people than ever before. It's a great time to be alive.

Here's a sampling of the top commercial pun-makers of the last fifty years ...

LOONY TUNES AND MERRIE MELODIES

In the 1930s a producer named Leon Schlesinger took an idea to Warner Brothers for a 'talk-ink' cartoon character. Luckily for us, they went for it, and Scheslinger put together a team of writers, animators and performers who made the world safe for puns. Paranomaniacs like Bugs Bunny, Daffy Duck, Porky Pig and Tweety Bird were created by an amazing bunch of eccentrics. Mel Blanc provided most of the voices, Carl Stalling played havoc with the soundtrack, and Tex Avery, Chuck Jones, Robert Mckimson, Bob Clampett and Friz Freleng laid the puns on thick. Their cartoon characters became household names and are still punning strong, sixty years later. While the work produced by Disney was better prepared and *looked* classier, the Warners' reels always got the laughs, and puns had a lot to do with it. In fact the only known pun associated with Walt Disney is one he uttered just before going into cryogenics, 'Have an ice day.'

Bugs Bunny would have to be the punsters' mascot, with lines like the one he chucked at the bull: 'What a maroon, what a nincowpoop!' But if it's puns you're after, you need look no further than the cartoons' titles: FRESH HARE, PIGS IN A POLKA, HISS AND MAKE UP, PECK UP YOUR TROUBLES, OF THEE I STING, SLICK HARE, WISE QUACKERS, CURTAIN RAZOR, HIS BITTER HALF, ROOM AND BIRD, HOME TWEET HOME, BIRD IN A GUILTY CAGE, I GOPHER YOU, LUMBER JERKS, HERE TODAY GONE TAMALE, and so on.

Those guys really went for it. Puns, anarchy, and a total lack of respect for authority. It's good to know we can still rely on some sources to be a good influence on our children.

ROY RENE

Roy Rene's character called 'Mo' was one of the most popular characters in Australia for over fifty years, constantly pushing the boundaries of good taste (whatever that is) with gags filled with puns. He hated the police and constantly baited them, which audiences loved, and it didn't hurt publicity either.

An example of his punning prowess pops up in a skit where Mo writes the letter 'F' on a blackboard and asks his faithful side-kick Stiffy to name it.

> Stiffy: K.
> Mo: No it's not. (He rubs it out and writes F again.)
>   What letter is it?
> Stiffy: It's the letter K.
> Mo: Try again, Stiffy. (He writes F again.) What letter is it?
> Stiffy: K.
> Mo: Why is it every time I write the letter F you see K?

Pretty outrageous stuff in those days, but so clever there was nothing the censors could do.

BILLY BIRMINGHAM

When the pun is consistently finessed *so* beautifully into scripts by another Australian, Billy Birmingham, you can see it for the rough diamond it is. In 'Australiana', he created a script of wall-to-wall puns performed by comedian Austen Tayshus, which went on to become the biggest selling local single ever. His inspired concept was to use Australian place names, flora and fauna, in a stoned monologue driven by the pun. Billy has said that it took only 45 minutes to write it, which suggests that he is the most natural-born-punster alive, or he can channel the ghosts of all the Marx Brothers at once. Dig some snippets of his masterpiece …

… Sittin' at home last Sunday morning and me mate Boomer rang, said he might kookaburra or two … great, Barry, a reefer … blue mountains away and his three sisters … how much can a koala bear? … She was trying to plait her puss … go, Anna … he'll definitely lead you astray, Liana …

Not just a flash in the pun, our Billy. His continuing ability to churn out funny lines in his 'Twelfth Man' recordings has put him firmly in the lead of Australian humorists. The pun in Oz is alive and kicking under his guidance.

THE *CARRY ON* MOVIES

This amazingly successful series of farces belonged to the 'show lots of flesh and make crass gags' school of British humour. Beginning in 1958 with *Carry On Sergeant*, most of these films were written by Talbot Rothwell who had grown up watching the smutty, innuendo-driven music hall comics like Max Miller.

Every *Carry On* movie worked the same formula, with lots of bodily function jokes and a cast of characters that included the matronly female, the busty slut, the mincing fag, the slimy older bloke, and the wisecracking trickster. Give them some 'wink wink' names, show some cleavage, chuck in the puns and you're away. Here's a taste …

Patient:	I was once a weak man.
Matron:	Once a weak is enough for any man.

Matron:	I want to be wooed.
Patient:	You can be as wude as you like with me.

Patient:	Matron's round!
2nd Patient:	I don't care what shape she is.

Sergeant:	Fire at will!
Soldier:	Poor old Will. Why do they always pick on him.

Lord of the castle:	Infamy! Infamy! They've all got it in for me!

Officer:	Your rank?
Soldier:	That's a matter of opinion.

Neighbour:	They spoil their pet to budgery.

Young lady to Lord:	You've always had magnificent balls.

Maid:	Drink inflames the ardour.
Lusty Count:	The more you drink the 'arder it gets.

Cowboy:	We've had no luck talking peace with the Sioux. One moment it's peace on, next moment it's

peace off.

And this from the country that gave us Shakespeare. But they were obviously on to something because they made twenty-nine of the bloody things!

THE GOONS

Spike Milligan and Peter Sellers have said that S.J. Perelman was their mentor during the Goons period, and does it show! Their completely manic, irreverent and childish radio show became the benchmark for alternative humour during the dour post-war period in Britain. Our favourite Goon pun is:

> How do you start a pudding race?
> Sago!

The Goons are still popular today, and copies of their scripts in book form are consistent sellers.

BENNY HILL

Along with Frankie Howerd and Terry Thomas, Benny Hill was known as a 'patter merchant', taking the 'refined' British view of all things sexual and with the aid of puns, turning it into one of the most successful comedy shows of all time. In the grand tradition of the *Carry On* films, Benny performed a public service by exposing what was going on beneath the covers (considering how many members of parliament have been wearing bondage gear and getting spanked lately). He had his own dancers, Hill's Angels, who spent most of their time with their legs in the air while wearing skimpy seventies bikinis (brilliant choreography). And of course there were puns. One skit featured a music store with a sign on the front door: Gone Chopin, Bach in a minuet, try Handel. And who can forget the scene where the wealthy landowner interrogates his stablehand (Hill) about his horse:

> Landowner: Where's my horse?
> Benny shrugs.
> Landowner: I told you I wanted my horse shod!
> Benny winces as a shot rings out.

It's lowbrow, it's stupid, and you can't help laughing at jokes you can see coming a mile off.

JAMES BOND MOVIES

Absent from Ian Fleming's original books, puns are now a standard feature in every Bond film. How many times have you seen Roger Moore say something like 'shocking' after some villain gets electrocuted? Head to the Bond shelf at your local video store for your pun fix.

WOODY ALLEN

With a pedigree like Allen's, is it surprising that the man can pun? He learned his trade supplying gags to New York comedians then writing funny magazine stories. He was one of the phenomenally talented writers for Sid Caesar's *Your Show of Shows* along with Mel Brooks, Carl Reiner and Larry Gelbart to name a few. He did his stand-up routines on *The Tonight Show* and the rest is history. He actually *played* a pun (Dr Noah) in the dreadful Bond spoof, *Casino Royale*, and gave the pun a starring role in *What's Up Tiger Lily?* This was the B-grade Japanese police flick which he over-dubbed with his own script, peppered with puns, including the hoary old classic, 'Two Wongs don't make a right.' Perelman would have been proud of him.

Woody relies less and less on the pun in his movies, but occasionally returns to the fold as he did in *Annie Hall*. His character is paranoid that someone is baiting him for being Jewish. Woody says, 'I asked him if he likes the film. He said, "No. Jew?"'

GET SMART

One of the funniest sitcoms ever made. *Get Smart* spoofed all the serious spy shows like *Man from U.N.C.L.E.*, *Mission Impossible* and *I Spy* that were so popular during the sixties. And they did it with pun after pun. The show was blessed by having Buck Henry and Mel Brooks write the scripts, and they took the mickey out of Hollywood every chance they could. Once again, the titles let you know what you're in for: THE TREASURE OF C. ERROL MADRE, SATAN PLACE, SURVIVAL OF THE FATTEST, A SPY FOR A SPY, THE MILD ONES, WITNESS FOR THE PERSECUTION, SPY SPY BIRDIE, GREER WINDOW, VALERIE OF THE DOLLS, APES OF RATH, PHYSICIAN IMPOSSIBLE.

It's important to remember that no matter how good the gags, if the guy delivering them can't cut the mustard, they'll fall flat.

The scripts were great, but Don Adams' timing was perfect.

*M*A*S*H**

This exceptionally witty series took traditional hospital drama and turned it on its head, much in the style of the Marx Brothers, with Alan Alda taking Groucho's role. He even aped the great one's mannerisms on occasion. It's interesting to note that like Groucho's persona, Alda became less madcap and lecherous and more fatherly as time passed, so if you live with a punster there's hope for you yet. A little note for trivia lovers: the film on which the series is based was written by Ring Lardner Jr, whose dad was also a meister-punner and member in good standing of the Algonquin Round Table. It's definitely in the blood.

Larry Gelbart, the head of the script department, wrote with beauty and compassion, making fun of authority at every turn and often with puns. For example, two sergeants are brawling, and Father Mulcahy tries to break them up. One of the pugilists responds: 'Don't worry, Father, I'm just breaking the jawbone of an ass.' *M*A*S*H** is perenially in reruns, which should make any fan of the pun very happy.

FLYING HIGH AND COMPANY

Jerry and David Zucker, Jim Abrahams and Pat Proft are responsible for some very funny, low-bred movies involving sex, violence and bodily functions. And you guessed it, they regularly employ the pun. *Flying High*, *The Naked Gun* and *Police Squad* combined slap-schtick and corny wordplay to entertain millions of fans worldwide. Let's get straight to it.

In *Flying High*, Peter Graves plays Captain Over, the pilot of a passenger plane, who tries calling for help when the entire crew is struck down by food poisoning. He receives a call from the Mayo clinic which is interrupted by a call from a Mr Ham. You can hear it coming. He says to the operator: 'All right, give me Ham on five and hold the Mayo.' Later, an ex-pilot played by Robert Hays confronts a doctor (Leslie Nielsen) about the illness sweeping through the plane:

> Hays: Surely there's something we can do.
> Nielsen: I'm doing everything I can.
>   And stop calling me Shirley.

In the sequel, Captain Over is introduced to his flight crew which includes officers Dunn and Under, who had served with him before:

> Co-pilot: Both Dunn and I were over Under even though I was
>   under Dunn.
> Over: Dunn was over Under and I was over Dunn.

The success of the *Police Squad* TV series led to the hugely successful *Naked Gun* movies which starred Leslie Nielsen and Priscilla Presley. They really let the puns lead them by the nose in these scripts. For instance, after his side-kick is shot, Nielsen goes down to the wharves to view the scene of the crime with partner George Kennedy:

Nielsen: Where did you find him?

Kennedy: Out there. (He points to the harbour.) Do you want to take a dinghy?

Nielsen: No thanks, I went before we left.

Later, Nielsen meets Presley who retrieves some files from the top of a bookshelf while he stands below:

Nielsen: Nice beaver!

Presley: Oh, thank you. I just had it stuffed. (She hands him down a mounted aquatic mammal.)

During their subsequent date, Nielsen tells of the death of his girlfriend in a tragic blimp accident:

Presley: Goodyear?

Nielsen: No, the worst.

You can see that the writers worked backwards, contriving their puns at the cost of logic and narrative context. But it's okay, as long as it's funny, right?

In the sequel, Nielsen and Kennedy go to a sex shop run by a woman with a suitably large cleavage:

Nielsen: Police, ma'am. We'd like to talk to you.

Woman: Is this some kind of bust?

Nielsen: Well, it's very impressive, but we need to ask you some questions.

The style of humour in these movies—sort of new age vaude-ville—is perfect for punning, and we can expect a lot more groan-worthy paranomasia from the same team in the future.

TELEVISION

The bland leading the bland.

Pure as the drivel show.

TRAVEL

Strangers On A Plane.
It Happened One Flight.

VIKINGS

The soft-spoken Viking: The Norse Whisperer.

WAR

The land mine took off his legs, so he laid down his arms.

One of the advantages of nuclear warfare
is that all men are cremated equal.

WIMPS

The meek shall inherit the hurt.

The shy who came in from the bold.

WINDSCREEN CLEANERS

Most of them must have seen the movie, Smear Window.

WORLD AFFAIRS

Britons will never be slaves, only Europe peons.

Shouts heard off the Adriatic: You go, Slavia!

WRITERS

A critic is a man who pans for gold.

A guy with writer's block is a man of few works.

A writer puns for gold.

An erratic poet writes the best and the versed.

Untalented grunge writer is a rebel without a clause.

If you have a decent idea, strike while the irony is hot.

Writer holding a gun to the head of a producer: make my play.

Book about witty repartee: Of Human Badinage.

Deadline: all word and no play.

Writer responding to a negative theatrical review:
before you judge me, you should walk a mile in my shows.

Hanging around with poets: bard company.

Authors' autobiographies are the best
because they're in their own write.

Newspapers sometimes have to fire their
shitty writers by taking out the pen dicks.

When the writer has to re-write something as a comedy
rather than a drama, she has to do an about farce.

The editor told the writer his stuff sucked, chapter and worse.

But the novelist defended himself: it could be verse.

THE FINAL
FRONTIER

New outlets and sources for puns are being developed all the time. One of the biggest growth areas is the Internet where electronic information is spreading the gospel, not all of it holy. The Net is becoming a kind of pun petrie dish, thanks to a shadowy group of Pun Eggheads. These people actually spend much of their life trying to find serious platforms for strange sub-categories of punning. They're a splinter group, unaffected by the major pun-players, and they don't have real jobs. Most of what they're into isn't serious academia, and it's definitely not funny. They are commonly found in university libraries, taking up enormous amounts of on-line time finding other Eggheads and asking questions like,

'Does anyone have any information relating to the naive interpretation of English by Japanese Businessmen?' Sure enough, replies come flooding back about useless golfers with uncontrollable flatulence, all in pun terms. Breathtaking in its intensity. These people are so weird they're giving the rest of us punsters a good name, if that's possible.

In addition to this pit of pun quicksand, there are a number of truly awful web sites devoted to puns. They are so bad we gave up trying to find a pun guru that we could consult without shaking our heads so often we had to see a chiropractor. Rent an old Marx Brothers movie instead, if you need a pun blast.

A great debate is raging about whether or not computers will ever be able to pun on their own. Sure, they can occasionally beat Kasparov at chess, but we suspect that it will be very hard to write a punning program which won't merely substitute one similar word for another. That would just be bad punning. Say, for instance, you type in the line, 'Beauty's only skin deep' and ask the program to make a pun, it might come up with something like, 'Beauty's only skin deed' or 'Beauty's only spin deep.' Meaningless. It's the subtle nexus of meanings on unlikely and humorous levels which will elude the computer chip. Of course, you might say that a computer can't fart or blow chocolate milk through its nose either, so what? But that would be getting off the point. In matters punnical, we refute the hypothesised supremacy of artificial intelligence.

Of course everyone who uses a computer is familiar with the ghost-in-the-machine type malapropism which can be very amusing and even relevant, although entirely unplanned by either you or your program. These words usually appear when you're going at it like a lunatic and late for a deadline. Inevitable when you tip slo quickly through the two lips.

Computers, however, are merely an accessory. Puns have always come and will always come from the minds of sick individuals. And with the help of this book, maybe there will be more of us around. We envision a new world order for the future. A global state with the punster as its standard bearer. Strong. Secure. Funny. Genghis Khan with a sense of humour. Wars will be fought by smarmy guys with drinks in their hands. The ruling junta could keep the masses down by making jokes only *they'd* get, libraries would become churches, churches would become bars, drugs would be legal, no sex act too disgusting. A Brave New Word.

THE PUNNING
HALL OF FAME

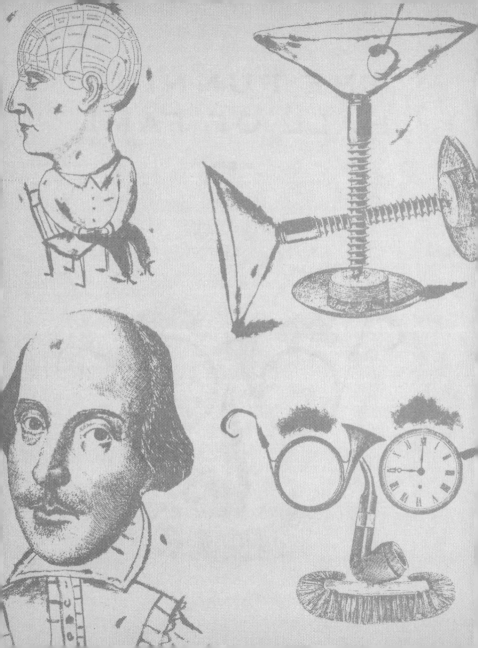

AESCHYLUS
For punning in ancient Greek. *We* can't do that.

EDWARD ALBEE
For the punning title of his finest play, *Who's Afraid of Virginia Woolf?*

FRED ALLEN
For being funny, and for succintly expressing the paradox of the pun.

DON ANDERSON
Australian writer and academic, for cancelling his subscription to the *Times Literary Supplement,* partly because they mangled one of his more rococo puns.

ARISTOTLE
For using the pun wisely and widely.

TEX AVERY
For making cartoons screwball. And using puns. God bliss him.

F.A. BATHER
For counting Shakespeare's puns and then analysing them statistically. Must've been single.

CHARLES-PIERRE BEAUDELAIRE
For poetically punning, and for experimenting with hashish in the investigation of pun-production.

SAMUEL BECKETT
For being a deathly funny existential punster, and using word-play to challenge things like Love and Truth and God.

HILAIRE BELLOC

For writing: When I am dead, I hope it may be said, His sins were scarlet, but his books were read.

BRENDAN BEHAN

For behan one of Ireland's highest-flying punning bad boys.

ROBERT BENCHLEY

The great writer and actor whose love affair with the bottle sent him down the path taken by many punsters.

JACK BENNY

For bridging the gap between vaudeville, movies and television with puns.

THE MARQUIS DE BIÈVRE

For resisting suggestions that he don the jacket with the sleeves that tie at the back, long enough to write a play with a pun in every line.

BILLY BIRMINGHAM

For using the pun in such a distinctly Australian way.

MEL BROOKS

Get Smart, Young Frankenstein, Blazing Saddles. Some pedigree.

ANTHONY BURGESS

For explaining many of James Joyce's and Lewis Carroll's trickiest paragrams, and for writing books like *A Clockwork Orange* which catapulted puns into the twenty-first century before we got there.

LORD BYRON
For his romantic puns, and all that bad behaviour.

GUILLERMO CABRERA INFANTE
For his dark, dense, disoriented Cuban punsters in *Three Trapped Tigers*.

SID CAESAR
His *Your Show of Shows* launched the careers of some of the funniest punsters the world has ever seen.

JIM CAPALDI
For his album titled, 'Whale Meat Again'.

LEWIS CARROLL (C.L. DODGSON)
Author of *Jabberwocky*, *Alice in Wonderland*, and *Alice Through the Looking Glass*. A first-class pervert, poet, punster.

THE *CARRY ON* MOVIES
The breast of British humour.

BENNETT CERF
For never outgrowing an utterly puerile love of dumb puns.

CHAUCER
For all those wilde and crayze punns in Middle Englishe.

CICERO
For amusing the ancient Romans with his ingenious, complicated and rewarding puns on bestiality.

BOB CLAMPETT

For putting puns in the mouth of Tweety—that sadist with yellow feathers. And what kind of mind gives Porky Pig that personality?

SAMUEL TAYLOR COLERIDGE

For doing all that opium while he wrote 'Kubla Khan', and for his love of puns.

JOHN DONNE

For re-inventing poetry, being seriously ahead of his time, and for using puns profusely and profoundly.

TED EGAN

For calling his Alice Springs property Sinkatinny Downs.

SERGEI EISENSTEIN

For articulating the link between verbal and visual puns.

EURIPIDES

For getting funny with the pun.

GUSTAVE FLAUBERT

For his genius and his puns.

H.W. FOWLER

For defending the pun in the *Dictionary of Modern English Usage*.

BENJAMIN FRANKLIN

For his generous and clever use of the pun in serious, nation-founding speeches and documents.

FRIZ FRELENG
Try and imagine a world without Bugs Bunny.

SIGMUND FREUD
For recognising the psychological importance of the pun.

ROBERT FROST
For making scared crows out of sacred cows.

LARRY GELBART
For writing some of the funniest modern puns in one of the best TV comedies ever, *M*A*S*H*.

JOHANN WOLFGANG VON GOETHE
For the amazing breadth of his work, and for being a very subtle punmeister.

GEORGE HARRISON
For the line which he supposedly ad-libbed in *A Hard Day's Night* when an interviewer asked him whether he was a 'mod' or a 'rocker', and he said, 'I'm a mocker.'

BUCK HENRY
For consistently excellent puns.

HERMES
For being the God of Punning, and lending his name to that really beautiful, expensive range of leather goods.

BENNY HILL
For keeping abreast of British humour.

OLIVER WENDELL HOLMES

Doctor, poet, punster, for attacking Calvinism when you could have your nuts cut off for doing so, and for punning in spite of his Draconian attempts at self-censorship.

THOMAS HOOD

The grand Victorian punster, for poetry like 'Faithless Sally Brown':

> His death, which happened in his berth,
> At forty-odd befell:
> They went and told the sexton, and
> The sexton toll'd the bell.

VICTOR HUGO

For waxing lyrical about the pun in *Les Miserables*.

EUGENE IONESCO

For the absurdity, paradox and ambiguity he expressed through the pun.

KING JAMES I (OF ENGLAND)

For rewarding punsters with big-time titles and significant fiefdoms.

CHUCK JONES

For being a real visionary. If you don't believe us, watch *Duck Dodgers in the 24 1/2 Century, What's Opera, Doc?* etc.

JESUS CHRIST

For founding Christianity on a pun.

BEN JONSON

For being one of the more outrageous Elizabethan punsters.

JAMES JOYCE

For being the Captain Kirk of the pun and taking it where no man had gone before, in *Ulysses* and especially *Finnegans Wake*. A photo-finish with Shakespeare in the race for the greatest punster of all time. Jim, we salute you.

CARL GUSTAV JUNG

For not only recognising the pun, but for using it and general wordplay to penetrate the deep hidden caverns of the unconscious.

JUVENAL

For keeping the punning faith in ancient Rome.

GEORGE S. KAUFMAN

For his cornucopia of neuroses, for putting up with the Marx Brothers, and for his puns.

JOHN KEATS

For punning on his deathbed.

RING LARDNER

For his wise and witty use of the pun in all his work, especially the story, 'Gullible's Travels'.

EDWARD LEAR

For his Victorian nonsense puns.

JOHN LENNON

For his many rude and psychedelic puns, especially the line that goes, 'A penis is a warm gun'. At least that's the way *we* heard it.

KATHY LETTE

For shamelessly punning when it's not really the 'literary' thing to do.

LUCRETIUS

For making puns which were as diverting as a Christian at lion-feeding time.

CHRISTOPHER MARLOWE

Along with Shakespeare and Ben Jonson, he made the Elizabethan world safe for punsters.

CHICO MARX

For responding to the line, 'Eureka!' with 'You doan smella so gooda youself.'

GROUCHO MARX

For embodying everything that is indulgent, abrasive, abusive and base about puns.

HARPO MARX

For keeping his wordplay off the screen and to himself. Unlike most punsters, he died happy.

HERMAN MELVILLE

For lines like this one from *Billy Budd*:

> O, 'tis me, not the sentence they'll suspend.

HENRY MILLER

For his porn puns, and for being b-b-b-b-b-bad to the bone.

SPIKE MILLIGAN

The master of tongue-fu.

JOHN MILTON

For including hundreds of puns in *Paradise Lost*. The devil made him do it.

JIM MORRISON

For writing the line, '... cause she's a twentieth-century fox ...'

VLADIMIR NABOKOV

For his palinlogues, anagrams, and puns, for creating the first Russian crossword puzzle, and for describing a character as wearing a Doppler shift.

FRIEDRICH NIETZSCHE

For being a visionary linguistic theorist, lunatic and promoter of the überpun.

GEORGE ORWELL

For using the pun to tell both sides of the story.

OVID

For coming up with puns that were as much fun as a chariot race.

DOROTHY PARKER

For being the one goddam stand-out female to hit the heights of punning with frequency, sophistication and wit.

ERIC PARTRIDGE

For being a great scholar and chronicler of wordplay in all its forms.

S.J. PERELMAN

For being the most influential and natural-born popular punster of the twentieth century.

PLATO
For teaching Aristotle that it was good to pun.

EDGAR ALLAN POE
For being as dark and weird as punsters get.

ALEXANDER POPE
For being a great, but diminutive, hunchback punster.

THOMAS PYNCHON
For using puns on a grand scale in the tradition of Swift, Joyce and Burgess.

FRANÇOIS RABELAIS
For his satire, his coarseness, his addiction to the pun. An inspiration to Rabelais-rousers everywhere.

WALTER REDFERN
For dedicating way too many years to a serious analysis and a history of the pun.

ROY RENE
For his repulsive character, 'Mo', who cocked a snoot at the powers that be with masterful puns.

FRANKIE RUBENSTEIN
For chronicling Shakespeare's sexual puns.

SAKI
For his simple, stylish puns.

LEON SCHLESINGER
For giving the Warner Brothers cartoonists the freedom to be insane.

ROBERT J. SEIDMAN

For helping us to understand *Ulysses*, and for being a witty defender of the well-placed pun.

WILLIAM SHAKESPEARE

For being puns' Big Daddy. Thousands of his puns have for centuries kept the true, shocking meaning of his words veiled. A tie for first place with James Joyce.

R.B. SHERIDAN

For creating the character, Mrs Malaprop, who gave her name to millions of mis-users of the language.

SMASHING PUMPKINS

For the use of the term 'Mellon Collie' in an album title.

SOCRATES

For teaching Plato that punning was cool.

SOPHOCLES

For making deeply dramatic puns.

THE REVEREND W.A. SPOONER

Although he was not the first to do it, for giving his name to the wonderful phenomenon of transposing sounds to humorous effect.

CARL STALLING

For making musical puns in the Merrie Melodies and Looney Tunes.

LAURENCE STERNE

An Irish punster (what a surprise), for the panoply of paranomasia in *Tristram Shandy*.

JONATHAN SWIFT

Another Irishman (and a priest!), for being a dedicated promoter of the pun in classic tales like *Travels into Several Remote Nations of the World by Lemuel Gulliver*, full of scatology, micturation, and lots of dirty jokes.

HENRY D. THOREAU

For getting us back to nature through the pun-fest that is *Walden*.

VIRGIL

For punning even though he wasn't very good at it.

OSCAR WILDE

For using a pun in the title of his best known play.

WILLIAM BUTLER YEATS

For his sensuality, his symbolism, and his fluid paranomasia.

JERRY ZUCKER, JIM ABRAHAMS, DAVID ZUCKER AND PAT PROFT

For *Flying High*, *The Naked Gun* and *Police Squad*, all of which featured tasteless, pun-plastered scenes involving sex, violence and bodily functions.

GLOSSARY

ambiguity double or uncertain meaning

antanaclasis pun in which the same word is repeated with a different meaning

archetype idea or image that comes from our collective unconscious

asteismus a reply which re-interprets an earlier word to convey a different meaning; a kind of pun

carwichet archaic for 'pun'

catamite a boy kept for sodomy

cavil archaic for 'pun'

chiasmus repetition of two words in reversed order

cliché a hackneyed expression

clinch in boxing, too close to throw a punch; in romance, an embrace; also archaic for 'pun'

conundrum a riddle with a pun in the answer

deuteroscopy the second view; that which is seen the second time around; a hidden meaning

double entendre a phrase or word with two meanings

echolalia the meaningless repetition of words or phrases

egghead a nerdy intellectual

embolophrasia compulsive wordplay in the manic stage of manic-depressive psychosis

epanados chiasmus

equivoque antanaclasis

eschatology not to be confused with scatology, a theological doctrine regarding death and judgement

etymology the derivation (or study) of words

euphuism artificial, affected writing style

existentialism philosophy which stresses the importance of existence and the freedom and responsibility of the individual

Förster's Syndrome Witzelsucht

heteronym a word the same as another in spelling but different in sound

homograph a word spelled like another but with different meaning and origin

homonym/homophone a word like another in sound but not meaning

irony a figure of speech in which the surface meaning is the opposite of the intended meaning

linguistics philology

litotes expressing the affirmative by using the negative of its opposite

macaronic like a jumble or medley [no connection to elbow pasta]

malapropism silly, unintentional misuse of a word that sounds like the intended word; a kind of unintentional pun.

meld pun a pun made by overlapping two words

metathesis transposition of sounds in a word or words

micturate to urinate

nexus bond, connection

nictitate to wink

non sequitur statement that doesn't follow logically from a previous one

oneiric of, or belonging, to dreams

onomatopoeia formation of a word using sounds associated with the thing to be named

oxymoron figure of speech using apparently contradictory expressions; one who has contracted mad cow disease

palimpsest page on which the original writing has been erased or covered to make way for new writing

paradox an apparently self-contradictory statement

paragram pun created by changing one or more letters of a word

paranomania compulsive punning

paranomasia Greek term for pun

paronym paragram

paraphilia any form of sexual activity in which arousal is dependent on socially unacceptable stimulation

parapraxis a Freudian slip

pedant poorly toilet-trained strict adherer to formal rules

philology linguistics

pleonasm use of more words than are necessary

ploce equivoque

polyptoton repetition of a word in different grammatical form with the same meaning

polysemy existence of more than one meaning in the same word

portmanteau word made by combining two words

pun see Chapter Two

pundemonium state in which seemingly lawless chaos reigns, but puns make sense

pundigrion very weird archaic version of 'pun'

pundit expert

punnet/punkin/punlet wee pun

punster one who puns

quark one of several hundred subatomic particles which comprise matter, they exist in clusters of three and imply that nature is three-sided rather than dualistic. The word was invented by James Joyce and appears in *Finnegans Wake* in a song that goes, 'Three quarks for Muster Mark', quark meaning 'cheer', 'squawk', and 'turds'.

quibble archaic for 'pun'

rhetoric language designed to persuade

scatology study of or preoccupation with excrement or obscenity

semantic relating to the meaning and connotation of words

semiology/semiotics area of linguistics concerned with signs and symbols

shadow the aspect of our unconscious that makes us pun unintentionally

solecism a breach of standard speech

spoonerism intentional or unintentional transposition of first consonants in two words eg. shap shot

Stolichnaya/Stoly really nice Russian vodka useful in motivating linguistic exercise (note well: keep in the freezer)

syllepsis zeugma

symbiosis association of two organisms living attached to each other

syntax sentence construction; how words are arranged grammatically

Tom Swifty awkward, punning abuse of an adverb with humorous intent

trickster the aspect of the self that makes us pun intentionally

trope a figure of speech

Witzelsucht embolophrasia

zeugma figure of speech applying one word to two others in different senses

BIBLIOGRAPHY

Adamson, Joe *Groucho, Harpo, Chico and Sometimes Zeppo*, W.H. Allen, London, 1973

Addison, Joseph *The Spectator*, no. 61, 10 May, 1711, London

Bather, Dr F.W. F.R.S., *Noctes Shakespeariance*, Winchester College, 1887

Beckett, S. *Breath and Other Shorts*. Faber & Faber, London, 1971

—— *Collected Poems*. J. Calder, London, 1984

Beckett, Samuel *Murphy*. Grove, New York, 1952

Benstock, B. *Joyce-Again's Wake*. University Press, Seattle, 1965

Bierce, A. *The Enlarged Devil's Dictionary*. Gollancz, London, 1867

Blamires, Harry *The Bloomsday Book: A Guide Through Joyce's Ulysses*. Methuen & Co., London, 1966

Bramwell, Murray & Matthews, David *Wanted for Questioning*. Allen & Unwin, Sydney, 1992

Burgess, Anthony *A Clockwork Orange*. Heinemann, London, 1962

—— *Joysprick: An Introduction to the Language of James Joyce*. Deutsche, London, 1973

—— *ReJoyce*. W.W. Norton & Co., London, 1965

Campbell, Joseph & Robinson, Henry Morton *A Skeleton Key to Finnegans Wake*. Viking Press, New York, 1947

Carroll, Lewis *Alice's Adventures in Wonderland*. dilithium Press, New York, 1988

—— *Alice Through the Looking Glass*. Australian Broadcasting Company (sound recording), Sydney, 1989

Chomsky, Noam *Reflections on Language*. Pantheon Books, 1975

Coleridge, Samuel Taylor *Anima Poetae*. ed. E. Coleridge, Heinemann, London, 1895

Crosbie, John S. *Crosbie's Dictionary of Puns*. Futura Publications, London, 1977

Davison, P.H. *Encyclopaedia Britannica*, 'Popular Literature'. 15th edn, vol. 14

Donne, J. & Smith, A.J. *The Complete English Poems of John Donne*. Penguin, Harmondsworth, 1971

Ellmann, Richard (ed.), *Selected Joyce Letters*. Viking Press, New York, 1975

—— *Ulysses on the Liffey*. Faber & Faber, London, 1972

Elwin, W. (ed.), *The Works of Alexander Pope*. Murray, London, 1886

Empson, W. *Seven Types of Ambiguity*. Penguin, Harmondsworth, 1973

Fieldhouse, Harry *Everyman's Good English Guide*. J.M. Dent & Sons Ltd, 1982

Freud, Sigmund *Jokes and Their Relation to the Unconscious*. The Hogarth Press and the Institute of Psycho-Analysis, 1905

—— *The Psychopathology of Everyday Life*. Penguin, Harmondsworth, 1975.

Gale, Steven & Grant, Thomas *American Humorists*. Stanley Trachtenberg ed., A Bruccoli Clark Book, Detroit, Michigan, 1982

Gifford, Don with Seidman, Robert J. *Notes for Joyce*. E.P. Dutton & Co., New York, 1974

Gilbert, Stuart *James Joyce's Ulysses*. Faber & Faber, London, 1930

Goldstein, J.H. & McGhee, P.E. *The Psychology of Humor*. Academic Press, New York, 1972

Gomez, V. Lothrop, *Wags to Witches*. Lee & Shepard Books, New York, 1981

Gross, J. *Joyce*. Fontana/Collins, London, 1971

Gruner, C.R. *Understanding Humor: The Working of Wit and Humor*. Nelson-Hall, Chicago, 1978

Halliwell, Leslie *Halliwell's Filmgoer's Companion*. Granada, London, 1983

Herrman, Dorothy *S.J. Perelman*. Simon & Schuster, London, 1986

Hughes, P. & Hammond, P. *Upon The Pun, Dual meanings in words and pictures*. W.H. Allen, London, 1978

Jones, Judy & Wilson, William *An Incomplete Education*. Ballantine Books, New York, 1987

Joyce, James *Finnegans Wake*. Faber & Faber, London, 3rd edn, 1964

—— *Ulysses*. (The Corrected Text) Bodley Head, London, 1986

Jung, Carl (ed.), *Man and His Symbols*. Dell Publishing, 1964

Larsen, E. *Wit as a Weapon*. Muller, London, 1980

LeComte, Edward *A Dictionary of Puns in Milton's English*. Macmillan Press, 1981

Legman, S. *Rationale of the Dirty Joke*. Grove Press, New York, 1982

Mahood, Molly *Shakespeare's Wordplay*. Methuen, London, 1979

McLuhan, Marshall & Carpenter, E. *Explorations in Communication*. Beacon Press, Boston, 1960

Milton, John *Paradise Lost*. Penguin, London, 1990

Nabokov, Vladimir *Lolita*. Weidenfeld & Nicolson, London, 1959

Nilsen, D.L. & Nilsen, A.P. *Laughing Play: An Introduction to Linguistics*. Newbury House, Rowley, Mass., 1978

Partridge, Eric *A Dictionary of Slang and Unconventional English*. Routledge & Kegan Paul, London, 1966

—— *Shakespeare's Bawdy.* Routledge & Kegan Paul, 1968

Poe, Edgar Allan *Works.* Ed. by E.C. Stedman and G.E. Woodberry, Stone and Kimball, Chicago, 1896

Pynchon, Thomas *Gravity's Rainbow.* Viking, New York, 1973

Quinn, Arthur *Figures of Speech.* Peregrine Smith, Salt Lake City, 1982

Raleigh, W. (ed.), *Johnson on Shakespeare.* Frowde, London, 1908

Raskin, V. *Semantic Mechanisms of Humor.* D. Reidel, Boston, 1985

Redfern, Walter *Puns.* Basil Blackwell Pub. Ltd., London, 1984

Ricks, C. Milton's *Grand Style.* Clarendon, London, 1968

Rubenstein, Frankie *A Dictionary of Shakespeare's Sexual Puns.* Macmillan Press Ltd, 1984

Sandulescu, Constantin-George *The Language of the Devil: Texture and Archetype in Finnegans Wake.* Gerrards Cross, Buckinghamshire, 1987

Schwarz, Daniel R. *Reading Joyce's Ulysses.* St. Martin's Press, New York, 1987

Shakespeare, William *The Complete Works of William Shakespeare.* Walter J. Black, New York, 1937

Smith, Sydney *Elementary Sketches of Moral Philosophy.* Longman, London, 1850

Swift, Jonathan *Gulliver's Travels.* J.M. Dent & Sons, London, 1973

Terban, Marvin *Funny You Should Ask.* Clarion Books, New York, 1992

Turner, G.W. *Stylistics.* Penguin, Harmondsworth, 1975

Vetter, H. *Language Behavior and Psychopathology.* Rand McNally, Chicago, 1969

Williams & Wilkins, *Stedman's Medical Dictionary.* Baltimore, 1966

Winokur, Jon *The Portable Curmudgeon.* New American Library, New York, 1987

Ziv, Avner (ed.), *National Styles of Humor.* Greenwood Press, Westport, Conn., 1988